ULTIMATE
GREEK GODS
HEROS &
VILLAINS

GREEK MYTHOLOGY COLORING & FACT BOOK

BRILLIANT IMAGES, MYTHOLGICAL STORIES & FACTS

High Detail Illustrations & Mythical Stories

- Top Tips -
To Get The Best Out Of This Book

Thank you for purchasing this colouring book.

Colouring is a great way to relax and can be an effective activity to relieve stress & anxiety. We really want you to enjoy your experience, so we recommend that you remove any distractions, and just allow yourself to enjoy the calm of the moment. Let your creativity and imagination take over as you get lost in the world of these images, bringing them to life with your choice of colour.

The pages of this book work best with coloured pencils, they also allow for great shading & detailing, wet mediums can be used but should be done so sparingly.

Any of you amazing works can be easily cut out and framed.

Zeus
King Of The Gods
The Story Of His Birth & Rise To Power

According to the myth, Zeus's father, Cronus, had overthrown and defeated his own father, Uranus, to become the ruler of the cosmos. However, Cronus had heard a prophecy that one of his own children would dethrone him, just as he had done to his father. To prevent this, Cronus swallowed each of his children as they were born.

To save Zeus from this fate, his mother Rhea devised a plan. When Zeus was born, Rhea presented Cronus with a stone wrapped in swaddling clothes, which he promptly swallowed, thinking it was Zeus. Rhea then hid Zeus in a cave on Mount Dikte, in the care of the nymphs Adrasteia and Ida, and the divine goat Amalthea, who nourished him with her milk.

As Zeus grew up in secrecy, he became a strong and mighty god. Eventually he returned to confront his father so that he could free his siblings. To do this Zeus decided to exploit Cronus's inability to resist consuming anything that was presented to him. Using his charm and cunning, Zeus convinced Cronus that consuming a special potion would make him even more powerful and invincible. Intrigued by the prospect, Cronus drank the potion.

The potion was a poison that caused intense sickness that forced Cronus vomit, and Cronus began to regurgitate the contents of his stomach. One by one, Zeus's swallowed siblings—Hestia, Demeter, Hera, Hades, and Poseidon—were freed from their confinement within Cronus.

Eventually they all returned to challenge their father and fought against Cronus and the other Titans in a colossal battle known as the Titanomachy.

Clashing in a fierce struggle for power. Zeus, with his thunderbolts, played a pivotal role in the conflict. Ultimately, the Olympians emerged triumphant, imprisoning the Titans in the depths of Tartarus, a dark and gloomy realm of the underworld.

Zeus then became the ruler of Mount Olympus

Ares
God Of War
The Trojan War

In the epic Trojan War, Ares, the Greek god of war, played a significant role, siding with the Trojans against the invading Greeks led by Agamemnon. Ares revelled in the chaos and bloodshed of battle, embodying the brutal and relentless nature of warfare.

Ares actively participated in the conflict, inspiring the Trojan warriors with his presence and joining the fight on their behalf. Clad in fearsome armour and wielding his mighty spear, he revelled in the mayhem and destruction he unleashed upon the Greek forces.

His influence on the battlefield was felt by both mortals and gods alike. Ares encouraged the Trojans to fight fiercely, filling their hearts with the desire for victory. The god's presence instilled fear and awe in the minds of the Greeks, who recognised the destructive power he possessed.

Despite his ferocity, Ares faced setbacks during the war. In Homer's epic poem, the "Iliad," the Greek hero Diomedes, aided by the goddess Athena, managed to wound Ares with a spear. The divine intervention left Ares wounded and forced him to retreat from the battle, nursing his injuries on Mount Olympus.

Ares' involvement in the Trojan War highlighted his role as the embodiment of violence and warfare. While he initially brought strength and encouragement to the Trojan side, his defeat at the hands of Diomedes illustrated that even gods were not invincible.

This story showcases the tumultuous nature of war and the unpredictable fortunes of battle. Ares' presence in the Trojan War emphasises the destructive and chaotic aspects of conflict, while also revealing the limitations and vulnerabilities of even the most powerful deities.

Hera

Queen Of The Gods - Goddess Of Marriage & Childbirth
Relationship With Zeus & Hercules

Hera, was the sister and wife of Zeus, the king of the gods. Their union was meant to be a symbol of power and harmony, but their relationship was full of challenges.

Zeus's was famously unfaithful and one of his affairs was with a mortal woman named Alcmene. Zeus had disguised himself as her husband, Amphitryon, and he seduced Alcmene, that resulted in the birth of the great hero Hercules.

When Hera learned of the birth Hercules, Zeus's son, she became jealous & angry, and decided to make Heracles' life difficult and bring him great suffering.

Hera sent two serpents to kill the baby Heracles while he slept in his crib. However, the baby Heracles strangled the serpents with his bare hands.

As Heracles grew older, Hera continued to scheme against him. She caused him to have fits of madness which made him commit horrible acts on those close to him.

To atone for his actions, Heracles was sentenced to perform twelve labours as punishment. These labours were seemingly impossible tasks that he had to complete under the guidance of King Eurystheus.

Throughout Heracles' trials, Hera played a role behind the scenes, often obstructing his progress and causing additional challenges. However, Heracles displayed immense strength, cunning, and perseverance to overcome each labour and proving himself as one of the greatest heroes in Greek mythology.

Despite Hera's animosity towards Heracles, the hero eventually achieved immortality and was welcomed among the gods on Mount Olympus. This reconciliation marked the end of Hera's direct antagonism towards him.

Hephaestus
God Of Fire, Metalworking & Craftsmanship
The Creation of Pandora

Hephaestus, was renowned for his exceptional skill in creating magnificent works of art. Despite his talent, Hephaestus faced challenges in his personal life. He was born with a physical deformity, often depicted as a limp or being hunchbacked, which caused him to be rejected and mocked by the other gods, including his mother, Hera.

One day, seeking vengeance against Hera for her rejection, Hephaestus devised a cunning plan. He decided to create a beautiful and irresistible woman named Pandora. Hephaestus crafted Pandora with meticulous precision, endowing her with enchanting beauty and charm.

However, Pandora was more than just a stunning creation. Hephaestus imbued her with various qualities and attributes, both desirable and problematic, to ensure that she would bring chaos and suffering to humanity.

As Hephaestus worked on Pandora's creation, he bestowed upon her gifts from different gods and goddesses. Athena gave her intelligence and skill, Aphrodite granted her captivating beauty, and Hermes gifted her with deceit and cunning.

Once Pandora was complete, Hephaestus presented her to Zeus, the king of the gods. Zeus, intrigued by her allure, saw an opportunity to punish humanity for receiving the gift of fire stolen by Prometheus. Zeus ordered Pandora to be sent down to Earth, accompanied by a box (later referred to as Pandora's box) with strict instructions not to open it.

Hades
God Of The Underworld & Ruler Of The Dead
The Abduction of Persephone - The Creation Of The Seasons

Hades, became infatuated with Persephone, the daughter of Zeus and Demeter. One day, as Persephone was gathering flowers in a meadow, Hades seized the opportunity and emerged from the depths of the Underworld in his chariot.

With great speed and force, Hades snatched Persephone and brought her back to the Underworld against her will. As he descended into the darkness, the earth split open, revealing a great chasm that swallowed them both, closing behind them.

Persephone's abduction left her mother, Demeter, the goddess of agriculture and fertility, distraught and grief-stricken. Demeter searched frantically for her beloved daughter, neglecting her duties and causing crops to wither and die.

Zeus, seeing the devastation and hearing the pleas of both Demeter and the suffering mortals, intervened. He demanded that Hades release Persephone and return her to the surface.

However, Hades had a plan. He cunningly offered Persephone a pomegranate, knowing that if she consumed any food in the Underworld, she would be bound to it and would have to return.

Persephone, swayed by hunger and the sweet taste of the pomegranate seeds, ate a few of them. This sealed her fate, and she became bound to the Underworld for a portion of the year.

A compromise was reached. Persephone would spend six months of the year with Hades in the Underworld, during which time Demeter mourned and the earth experienced winter and barrenness. But when Persephone returned to her mother for the remaining six months, Demeter's joy would bring forth spring and abundance.

Thus, the story explains the cycle of the seasons, with Persephone's time in the Underworld symbolising winter, and her return to the surface marking the arrival of spring.

Artemis
The Goddess Of The Hunt & The Moon
The Story Of Artemis & Orion

Artemis, known for her fierce independence and dedication to the wild, roamed the forests and mountains with her band of loyal nymphs. Among her companions was Orion, a mighty hunter and warrior renowned for his strength and skill.

Artemis and Orion formed a deep bond, sharing a mutual love for the hunt and the wilderness. They would often venture together, tracking formidable creatures and exploring the uncharted realms of nature. Their friendship grew stronger with each adventure, and they became inseparable.

One day, during a peaceful gathering, a jealous and vengeful Apollo, Artemis's twin brother, intervened. Apollo was aware of his sister's deep affection for Orion and saw it as a threat to her vow of eternal maidenhood. Seizing an opportunity to create discord, Apollo approached Artemis with false claims, warning her of Orion's intentions to dishonour her. Deceived by her brother's words, Artemis became suspicious and decided to test Orion's loyalty.

As Orion swam in the vast ocean, Artemis unleashed a giant scorpion to attack him. The scorpion struck Orion with its venomous stinger, inflicting a fatal wound. Despite his valiant efforts, Orion succumbed to the scorpion's venom and faced imminent death.

Overwhelmed with grief and remorse, Artemis realised the truth and the extent of Apollo's deceit. She rushed to Orion's side, cradling him in her arms as he took his final breath. Filled with sorrow, Artemis decided to honour her fallen companion in the most enduring way possible.

Using her divine powers, Artemis elevated Orion's spirit to the heavens, transforming him into a brilliant constellation. Orion's figure, holding a mighty club and wearing a lion's pelt, became a permanent fixture in the night sky, serving as a reminder of their enduring friendship and the tragic consequences of deception.

From that moment on, Artemis pledged to protect and watch over the constellation of Orion, ensuring his eternal presence in the celestial realm.

Athena

Goddess Of Wisdom, Courage & Strategic Warfare
Athena Vs Poseidon - The Contest For Athens

When Athens was a young city, it was searching for a god to be patron, Athena and Poseidon decided that they would like the honour, and so a contest was held to decided the winner. Each would offer a gift to the city and the people of Athens would then decide the winner.

The contest began at the Acropolis, the sacred hill where the city would later flourish. Poseidon, god of the sea and earthquakes, struck his trident into the ground with great force. As he did, a spring erupted, water gushing forth in a powerful display. However, this water was saltwater, rendering it unfit for drinking or irrigation.

Next came Athena, goddess of wisdom, crafts, and strategic warfare. She knelt down and gently planted an olive tree into the earth. The tree quickly took root and grew with remarkable speed, its branches stretching out, providing shade and peace.

Observing Athena's gift, the people of Athens recognised its tremendous value. The olive tree offered sustenance, oil for lamps and cooking, and branches for shelter and crafting. It symbolised fertility, peace, and prosperity for the city. Impressed by the practical and bountiful nature of Athena's offering, the citizens declared her the victor and chose her as the patron goddess of Athens.

In honour of Athena's victory, the city was aptly named Athens, and the olive tree became a cherished emblem, adorning coins, sculptures, and temples throughout the city. Athena, grateful for the citizens' trust, became a guardian and protector of Athens, guiding its growth and providing wisdom to its people.

The contest for Athens serves as a testament to Athena's wisdom and practicality. Her gift of the olive tree showcased her ability to nurture and foster civilisation, while Poseidon's spring highlighted the untamed power of the sea. Ultimately, the citizens recognised Athena's contribution as more beneficial and aligned with their aspirations for a prosperous and peaceful city.

Griffin
Body Of A Lion - Head & Wings Of An Eagle
The Golden Fleece

In the epic quest for the Golden Fleece, When Jason and the Argonauts approached the destination of the Fleece they learned that it was guarded not only by a fierce dragon named Ladon but also by a pair of mighty griffins.

The griffins, creatures with the body of a lion and the head and wings of an eagle, were fearsome guardians of the Golden Fleece. Their imposing presence and powerful nature made them formidable adversaries for anyone seeking to claim the treasure.

Knowing the challenge that lay ahead, Jason sought the guidance and favour of the goddess Athena. With her assistance, he devised a plan to approach the griffins and persuade them to allow him to pass. Athena granted Jason the ability to communicate with animals. As Jason and his companions approached the griffins, he used this ability to speak to the majestic creatures & he conveyed his noble intent and his desire to retrieve the Golden Fleece for a just cause.

Impressed by Jason's courage and the honourable nature of his quest, the griffins decided to offer their support. They acknowledged the significance of the Golden Fleece and recognised Jason's worthiness to possess it. In a display of trust and cooperation, the griffins allowed him and the Argonauts to pass unharmed, granting them safe passage to face the dragon Ladon.

Hestia
Goddess Of The Hearth & Home
The Theft of Fire

In the tale of the theft of fire, Prometheus played a pivotal role in shaping the destiny of humanity. However, it was Hestia, the goddess of the hearth and home, who played a significant part in resolving the conflict that arose from this audacious act.

When Prometheus stole fire from the gods and bestowed it upon mortals, Zeus, the king of the gods, was enraged. He saw this act as a breach of divine authority and sought to punish Prometheus severely. However, Hestia, with her gentle and nurturing nature, stepped forward to advocate for a different course of action.

Recognising the vital importance of fire for the well-being of humanity, Hestia approached Zeus with compassion and wisdom. She spoke of the warmth and sustenance fire provided to mortals, allowing them to survive, thrive, and create civilisation. Hestia believed that taking away fire would only bring suffering and hardship upon humans.

Moved by Hestia's earnest plea and her deep understanding of the human condition, Zeus's anger was softened. Instead of a harsh punishment for Prometheus, Zeus decided on a more lenient sentence, with the intent of balancing justice and mercy.

Hestia's intervention showcased her devotion to the well-being of mortals and her role as the guardian of the hearth. She understood the fundamental need for warmth, nourishment, and domestic harmony within the human realm. Hestia's advocacy for compassion and her appreciation for the essential elements of daily life helped to shape the resolution of this conflict.

Hera

Queen Of The Gods - Goddess Of Marriage & Childbirth
The Creation of the Milky Way

The tale begins with the birth of Hercules, the son of Zeus and a mortal woman named Alcmene. Knowing that Hercules would possess great strength and potential, Zeus desired to grant him immortality by having him drink from Hera's divine milk. However, Hera, harbouring deep resentment towards Zeus' affairs and illegitimate children, refused to nurse the infant.

Seeing the importance of Hercules' destiny, Athena (Goddess Of Wisdom, Courage & Strategic Warfare) devised a plan take the baby Hercules to Hera, disguising him as an orphaned mortal, and pleaded with the queen of the gods to care for the infant.

Touched by the sight of the helpless baby, Hera's maternal instincts prevailed, and she reluctantly agreed to nurse him. Little did she know that this act would have a profound impact on the heavens.

As Hercules suckled at Hera's breast, the divine milk infused him with strength and immortality. However, Hera, sensing something extraordinary, pulled away abruptly, causing a few drops of her milk to spill across the night sky.

These celestial droplets formed a radiant trail that stretched across the heavens, creating the awe-inspiring phenomenon known as the Milky Way.

Apollo
God Of Music, Poetry, & Prophecy
Apollo & The Python

Apollo, the radiant god of music, poetry, and prophecy, encounters a fearsome serpent known as Python. Hera, queen of the gods sent the serpent to torment Apollo's mother, Leto, during her pregnancy.

Fuelled by a burning desire to avenge his mother, Apollo sets out on a quest to confront Python. The serpent had taken refuge in the sacred region of Delphi, where it wreaked havoc and instilled fear among the people.

With his bow and arrows in hand, Apollo embarks in a battle against Python. The clash between the god and the monstrous serpent is fierce and relentless. Apollo's arrows pierce Python's scaly hide, while the serpent thrashes and coils in an attempt to overpower his divine adversary.

After a gruelling struggle, Apollo prevails, delivering a fatal blow to Python. The serpent succumbs to the god's might, its enormous body falling lifeless upon the earth. The land is freed from the terror of Python's presence, and a triumphant Apollo stands victorious.

In recognition of his victory, Apollo establishes the Oracle of Delphi at the very site where Python fell. He appoints a priestess known as the Pythia to convey his divine messages and prophecies to those who seek guidance. The Oracle of Delphi becomes a revered sanctuary, drawing pilgrims from far and wide who seek Apollo's wisdom and foresight.

Pandora
The First Mortal Woman Created By The Gods

According to the myth, Zeus, the king of the gods, ordered Hephaestus, the god of craftsmanship, to mould Pandora, the first mortal woman out of clay. Then each of the gods bestowed upon her various gifts:

Beauty: Aphrodite, the goddess of love and beauty, granted Pandora unparalleled physical attractiveness. She was created with exceptional grace and charm, captivating all who beheld her.

Intelligence: Athena, the goddess of wisdom and warfare, bestowed upon Pandora intelligence and cunning. This gift provided her with the capacity for discernment and strategic thinking.

Craftsmanship: Hephaestus, the god of craftsmanship and fire, contributed to Pandora's creation by moulding her out of clay with great skill. His gift ensured that she was crafted with precision and artistry.

Musical Talent: Apollo, the god of music and poetry, gifted Pandora with a melodious voice and exceptional musical talent. She possessed the ability to enchant and captivate others through her singing.

Eloquence: Hermes, the messenger of the gods, granted Pandora the gift of eloquence. She was able to articulate her thoughts and express herself persuasively, possessing the gift of effective communication.

These gifts from the gods made Pandora a truly remarkable and enchanting figure. Her physical beauty, intellectual capabilities, musical talent, and eloquence made her an embodiment of divine qualities. However, it is worth noting that despite these gifts, Pandora's actions and the subsequent opening of the jar led to the release of misfortunes into the world, forever altering the human experience.

The Gorgon Medusa
Head Of Snakes & Petrifying Gaze
"Medusa's Curse"

Medusa was originally a beautiful maiden with long, golden hair. She caught the attention of Poseidon, the god of the sea, and they engaged in a romantic tryst inside Athena's temple.

Athena, the goddess of wisdom and warfare, was furious at this act of desecration and betrayal. In her anger, she transformed Medusa's beautiful hair into a writhing mass of venomous snakes. Medusa's once enchanting visage became terrifying, and her gaze had the power to turn any mortal who looked upon her into stone.

Athena's punishment for Medusa was severe and everlasting, as it not only altered her physical appearance but also isolated her from human society. Medusa was forced into a life of solitude, dwelling in a remote cave, away from the civilised world. Her monstrous form and lethal gaze made her an outcast, feared by all who encountered her.

The story of Medusa incurring the wrath of Athena adds layers of complexity to Medusa's character and explains the origins of her monstrous appearance. It emphasises the power of divine retribution and the consequences of defying the gods in Greek mythology.

Pandora's Box

The creation of Pandora's box is tied to the story of Prometheus and his theft of fire from the gods. Prometheus, known for his cunning and sympathy for humanity, desired to help mortals by providing them with the divine gift of fire, which would grant them warmth, light, and the ability to progress.

However, Zeus, the king of the gods, was furious at Prometheus for disobeying his command and stealing fire. Seeking revenge, Zeus devised a plan to punish both Prometheus and humanity. He ordered Hephaestus, the god of craftsmanship, to mould a woman named Pandora out of clay.

Zeus and the gods endowed Pandora with extraordinary beauty and bestowed upon her various seductive qualities. He then presented her as a "gift" to Epimetheus, Prometheus's brother. Despite Prometheus's warnings, Epimetheus fell captivated by Pandora's allure and accepted her as his wife.

After creating Pandora, Zeus gave her a mysterious box, known as Pandora's box, and gave strict instructions never to open it. However, curiosity overwhelmed Pandora, and her desire to explore the contents became insatiable.

Unable to resist any longer, Pandora opened the box, unleashing a multitude of miseries and evils upon the world. Out flew diseases, plagues, sorrows, and all the troubles that would plague humanity. Pandora, filled with regret, quickly closed the box, trapping one thing inside: hope.

While Pandora's action brought suffering and hardship, the presence of hope within the box offered solace and resilience. It became a symbol of the enduring spirit and optimism that humanity clings to even in the face of adversity.

Pegasus
The Winged Horse
Pegasus and Bellerophon

One of the most famous stories involving Pegasus is the tale of Pegasus and Bellerophon. Bellerophon was a skilled and courageous hero who sought to tame and ride the winged horse. With the help of Athena and Poseidon, who provided him with a magical bridle, Bellerophon successfully captured Pegasus.

Mounted on the back of Pegasus, Bellerophon embarked on various heroic adventures. Together, they defeated the monstrous Chimera, a fire-breathing creature with the body of a lion, the head of a goat, and the tail of a serpent. The triumphs of Bellerophon and Pegasus made them legendary figures in Greek mythology.

However, Bellerophon's pride grew, and he attempted to fly to Mount Olympus, the realm of the gods, on Pegasus's back. Zeus, angered by this audacity, sent a gadfly to sting Pegasus. Startled, the winged horse threw off Bellerophon, who fell to Earth and lived out his days in misery.

This story highlights the partnership between Pegasus and Bellerophon, showcasing the horse's incredible speed and strength. It also warns against hubris and the consequences of attempting to defy the gods.

Persephone
Daughter Of Zeus
The Eleusinian Mysteries

The story of the Eleusinian Mysteries begins with Persephone's abduction by Hades, the god of the underworld. While Persephone was gathering flowers in a meadow, Hades emerged from the earth in his chariot and whisked her away to his realm against her will. Demeter, devastated by her daughter's disappearance, caused the crops to wither and the Earth to plunge into an eternal winter.

Zeus, concerned by the suffering of humanity due to Demeter's grief, intervened and demanded the return of Persephone to the surface. However, Persephone had consumed six pomegranate seeds during her time in the underworld, binding her to Hades for a portion of the year.

Demeter, upon being reunited with her daughter, brought forth the return of spring and the renewal of life. To commemorate this reunion and to honour the trans-formative power of the goddesses, the Eleusinian Mysteries were established.

The Eleusinian Mysteries were secretive initiation ceremonies held in the city of Eleusis. These rituals were believed to provide spiritual enlightenment, purification, and the promise of a blessed afterlife. The details of the ceremonies remain shrouded in mystery, as participants were sworn to secrecy under penalty of death.

Persephone, as the bridge between the realms of life and death, played a significant role in these rites. Her journey to the underworld and subsequent return symbolised the cycle of life, death, and rebirth. The mysteries offered participants the hope of immortality and a connection to the divine.

The Eleusinian Mysteries became renowned throughout Greece, attracting initiates from all walks of life. It was believed that those who underwent the rituals would experience personal growth, spiritual transformation, and a deeper understanding of the mysteries of existence.

Hercules

Son Of Zeus

The Twelve Labours Of Hercules

12 labours were assigned to Hercules by King Eurystheus as punishment for killing his wife and children in a fit of madness.

1.

Slay the Nemean Lion: Hercules strangled the ferocious lion with his bare hands, as its golden fur was impenetrable to weapons.

2.

Slay the nine-headed Lernaean Hydra: Hercules defeated the Hydra by cutting off its heads, but faced the challenge of its regenerative abilities.

3.

Capture the Golden Hind of Artemis: Hercules caught the sacred deer after a year-long pursuit.

4.

Capture the Erymanthian Boar: Hercules captured the monstrous boar by driving it into deep snow.

5.

Clean the Augean stables in a single day: Hercules diverted rivers to cleanse the filthy stables of King Augeas.

6.

Slay the Stymphalian Birds: Hercules used a rattle gifted by Athena to scare the man-eating birds and shot them down.

Cont'd on Next Page

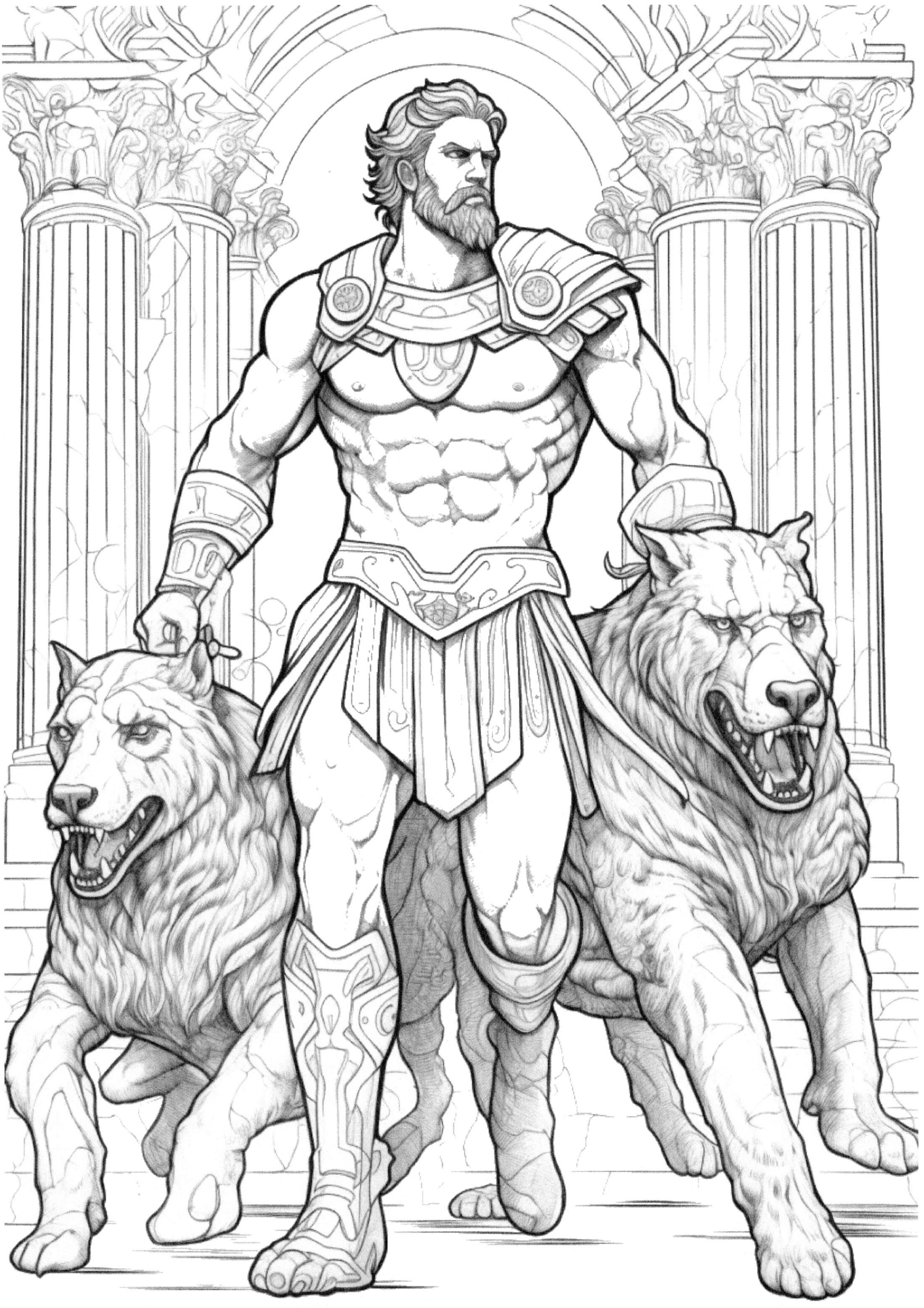

Hercules
Son Of Zeus
The Twelve Labours Of Hercules (cont'd)

7.

Capture the Cretan Bull: Hercules managed to wrestle the powerful bull into submission.

8.

Steal the Mares of Diomedes: Hercules stole the flesh-eating horses by feeding them their own master, Diomedes.

9.

Obtain the girdle of Hippolyta, the Queen of the Amazons: Hercules successfully negotiated with Hippolyta and received the girdle as a gift.

10.

Obtain the cattle of the monstrous Geryon: Hercules killed Geryon and drove the cattle back to Eurystheus.

11.

Steal the apples of the Hesperides: Hercules tricked Atlas into retrieving the golden apples from his daughters while he held the heavens.

12.

Capture and bring back Cerberus, the three-headed dog of the underworld: Hercules fought off the guardians and secured Cerberus, bringing him to the mortal realm before returning him to Hades.

Hercules overcame significant adversity and completed all 12 tasks and after gaining immortality and returning to mount Olympus it solidified his status as one of the greatest heroes in Greek mythology.

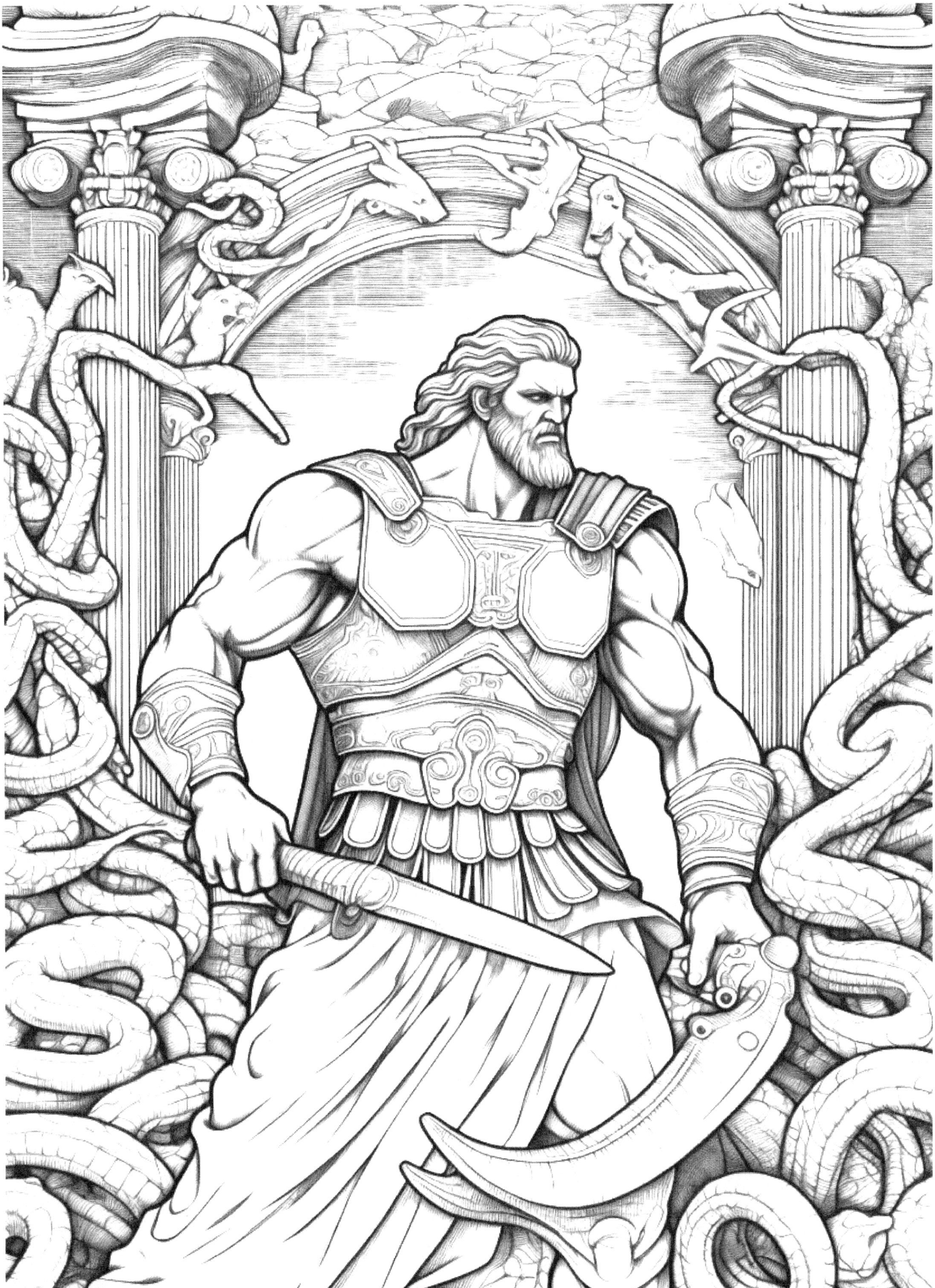

Dionysus
God Of Wine, Revelry & Ecstasy
Myth Of King Midas

Dionysus is in the myth of King Midas. Once, Dionysus, in a display of gratitude, granted King Midas a wish, allowing him to choose whatever he desired. King Midas, in his greed, asked for the ability to turn everything he touched into gold.

Initially delighted by his newfound power, King Midas soon realised the downside when he discovered that even food and drink turned into inedible gold. His daughter, terrified and hungry, became the catalyst for his change of heart. King Midas prayed to Dionysus, begging him to take back the golden touch.

Dionysus agreed to relieve King Midas of his curse, instructing him to cleanse himself in the river Pactolus. As the king did so, the curse was lifted, and everything he had turned to gold returned to its original form.

This story serves as a cautionary tale about the dangers of excessive greed and material wealth. It showcases Dionysus' power and his role in teaching mortals valuable lessons about moderation and contentment.

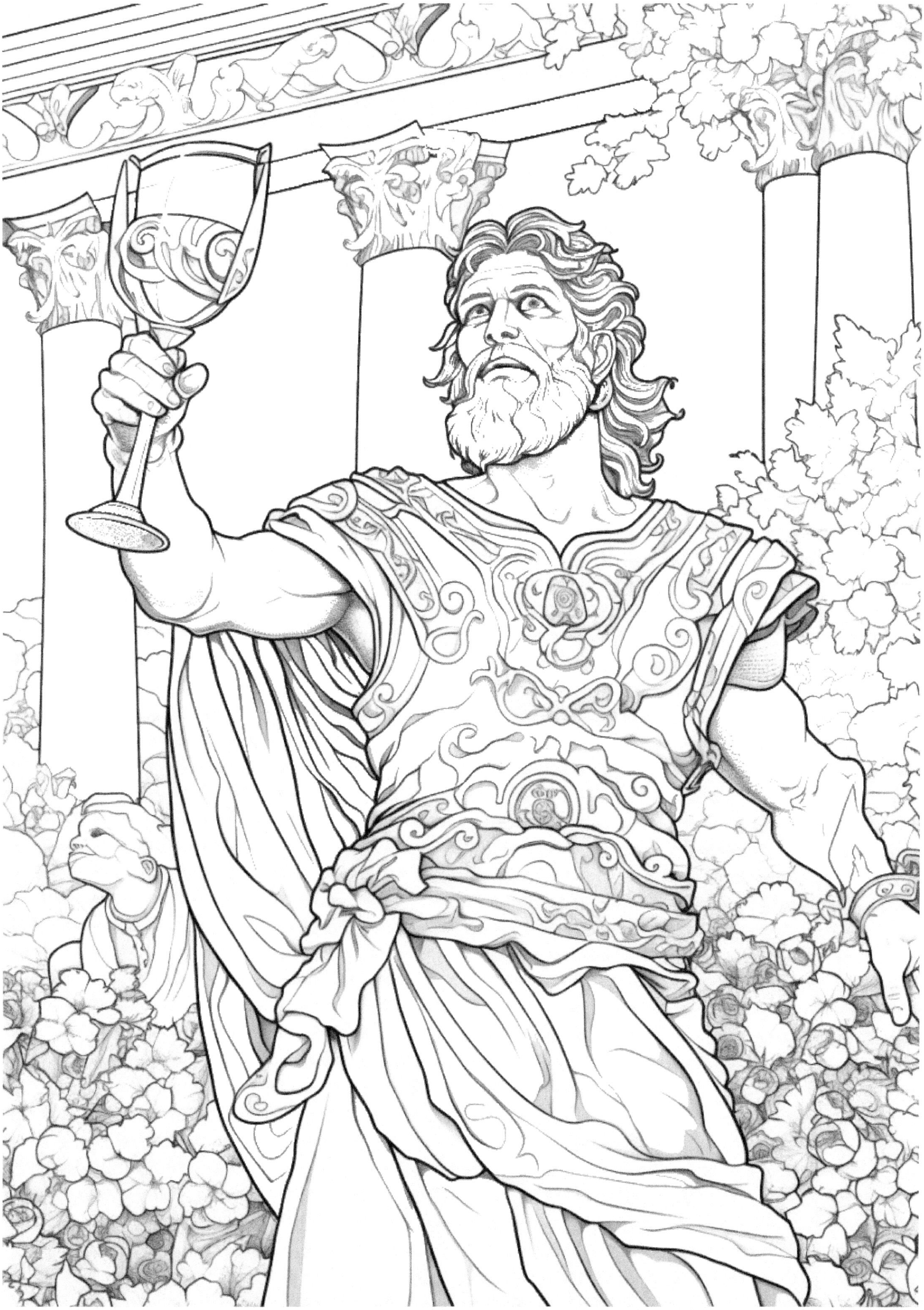

Hydra
Regenerating Mythical Monster
The Second Labour Of Hercules

In the second labour of Hercules. Heracles was tasked with slaying the monstrous Hydra, which lived in the marshes of Lerna. Each time one of the Hydra's heads was cut off, two new heads would grow in its place, making it a formidable opponent.

Heracles, accompanied by his nephew Iolaus, devised a strategy to defeat the Hydra. As Heracles engaged in combat, Iolaus used a burning torch to sear the neck stumps of the Hydra, preventing the heads from regenerating. With this strategy, Heracles was able to cut off each head and cauterise the wounds. Finally, he severed the immortal head and buried it under a heavy rock.

However, the Hydra had a poisonous blood that was deadly. Heracles dipped his arrows in the Hydra's blood, making them lethal weapons for future battles. The Hydra was vanquished, and Heracles successfully completed his second labour.

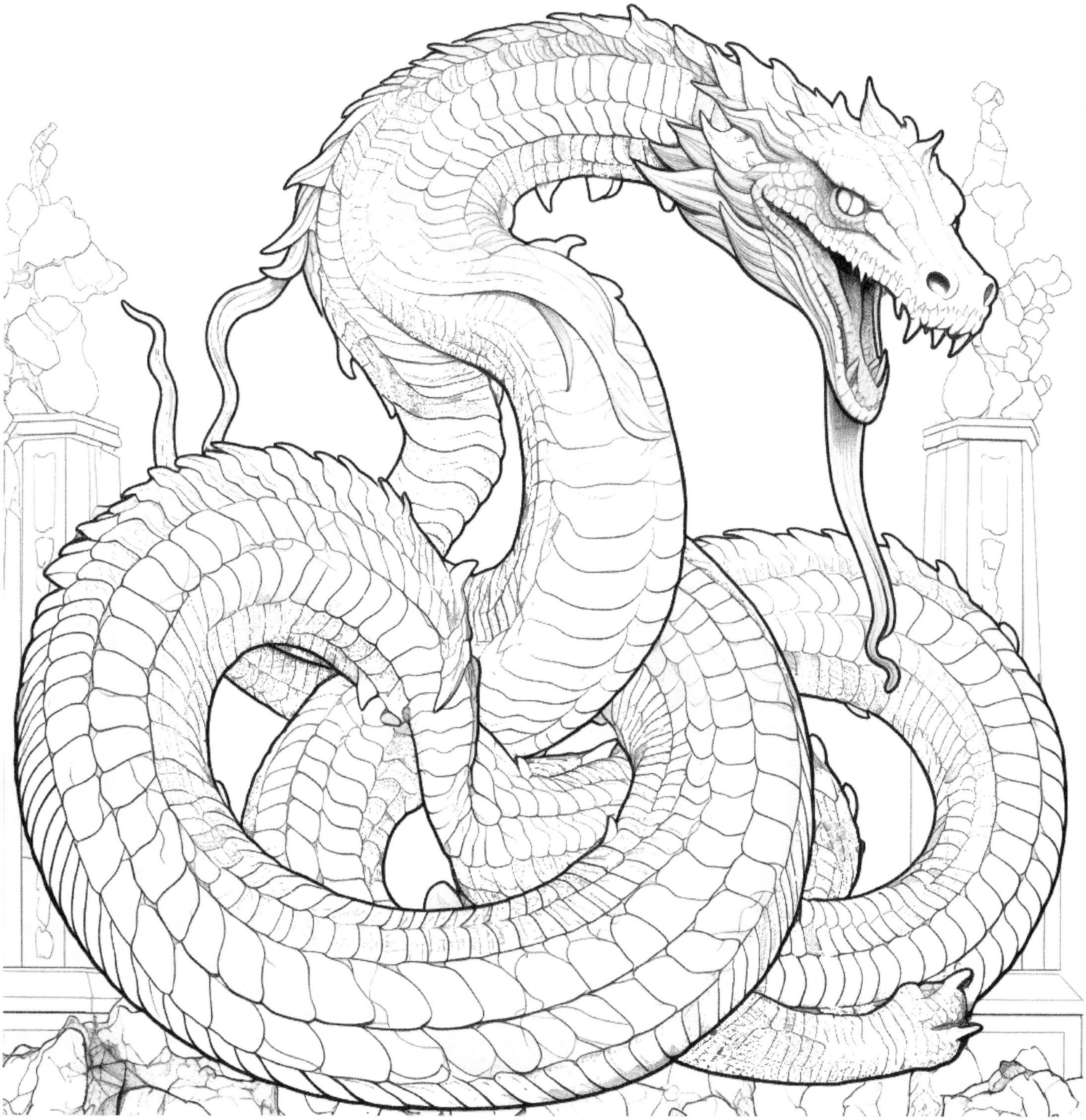

Demeter
Goddess Of Agriculture & Fertility
Demeter & The Gift Of Agriculture

Demeter, the Greek goddess of agriculture and fertility, played a vital role in bestowing the gift of agriculture upon humanity. She observed the struggles of mortals who relied solely on hunting and gathering for sustenance. Determined to improve their lives, she decided to share her knowledge and secrets of farming.

One day, Demeter chose Triptolemus, a young mortal prince, as the recipient of her gift. She appeared before him and taught him the art of cultivation, explaining the importance of sowing seeds, tending crops, and reaping bountiful harvests. To aid him in his mission, she bestowed upon him a magical chariot, drawn by magnificent winged serpents.

Triptolemus embarked on a remarkable journey across the world, spreading the wisdom of agriculture wherever he went. He taught people how to plow the fields, plant seeds, and cultivate various crops. With each stop on his journey, he shared Demeter's teachings, transforming barren lands into fertile fields.

The impact of Triptolemus' teachings was immense. Communities embraced agriculture as a way of life, recognising its ability to provide a stable food source, promote civilisation, and foster prosperity. Grateful for Demeter's gift, people honoured her as the patron goddess of agriculture, offering prayers and sacrifices to ensure bountiful harvests.

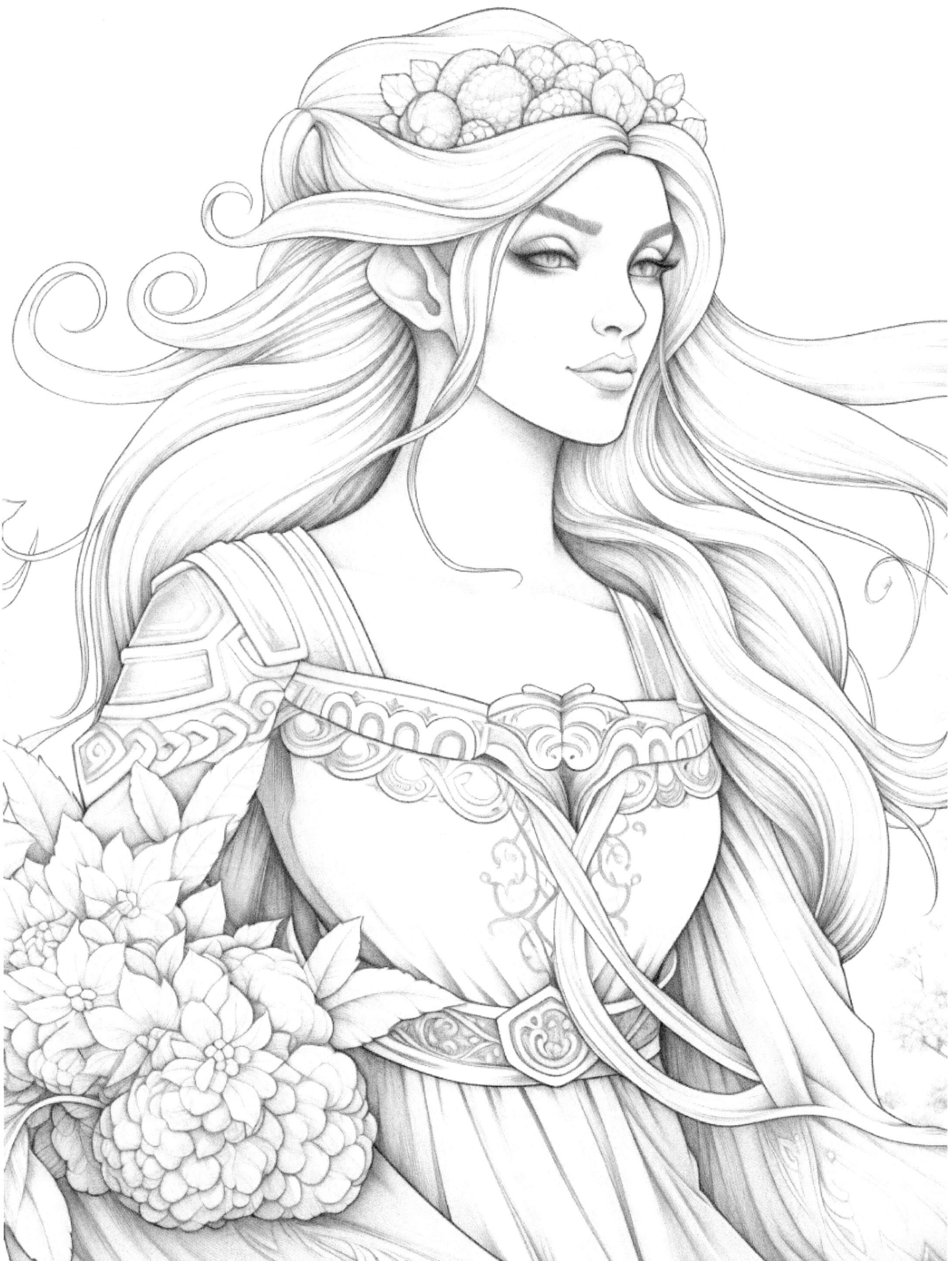

Achilles
Legendary Hero

Achilles, also known as Achilles of Phthia, was a legendary hero in Greek mythology. He was the son of the mortal Peleus, a king, and the sea nymph Thetis, who was a minor goddess. Achilles was known for his exceptional strength, bravery, and skill in battle. He was considered the greatest warrior of the Greeks during the Trojan War.

Achilles' most famous attribute was his invulnerability, except for his heel, which became his fatal weakness. According to the myth, when he was an infant, his mother Thetis dipped him in the River Styx, which made him invincible. However, she held him by the heel, leaving that area untouched by the water. This vulnerable spot on his body would later lead to his downfall.

During the Trojan War, Achilles fought on the side of the Greeks and played a crucial role in their battles against the Trojans. His rage and withdrawal from the war, due to a dispute with Agamemnon, caused significant setbacks for the Greek forces. However, his return to battle and subsequent slaying of Hector, the Trojan prince, demonstrated his fierce combat skills and desire for revenge.

Despite his prowess on the battlefield, Achilles met a tragic end. Paris, a Trojan prince, shot a poisoned arrow guided by the god Apollo, striking Achilles in the vulnerable heel, which led to his demise. His death marked the conclusion of the Trojan War and became a prominent theme in Greek literature and art.

Achilles' story embodies the themes of heroism, pride, and fate, showcasing both his exceptional abilities and his tragic flaw. His character has had a lasting impact on Western literature.

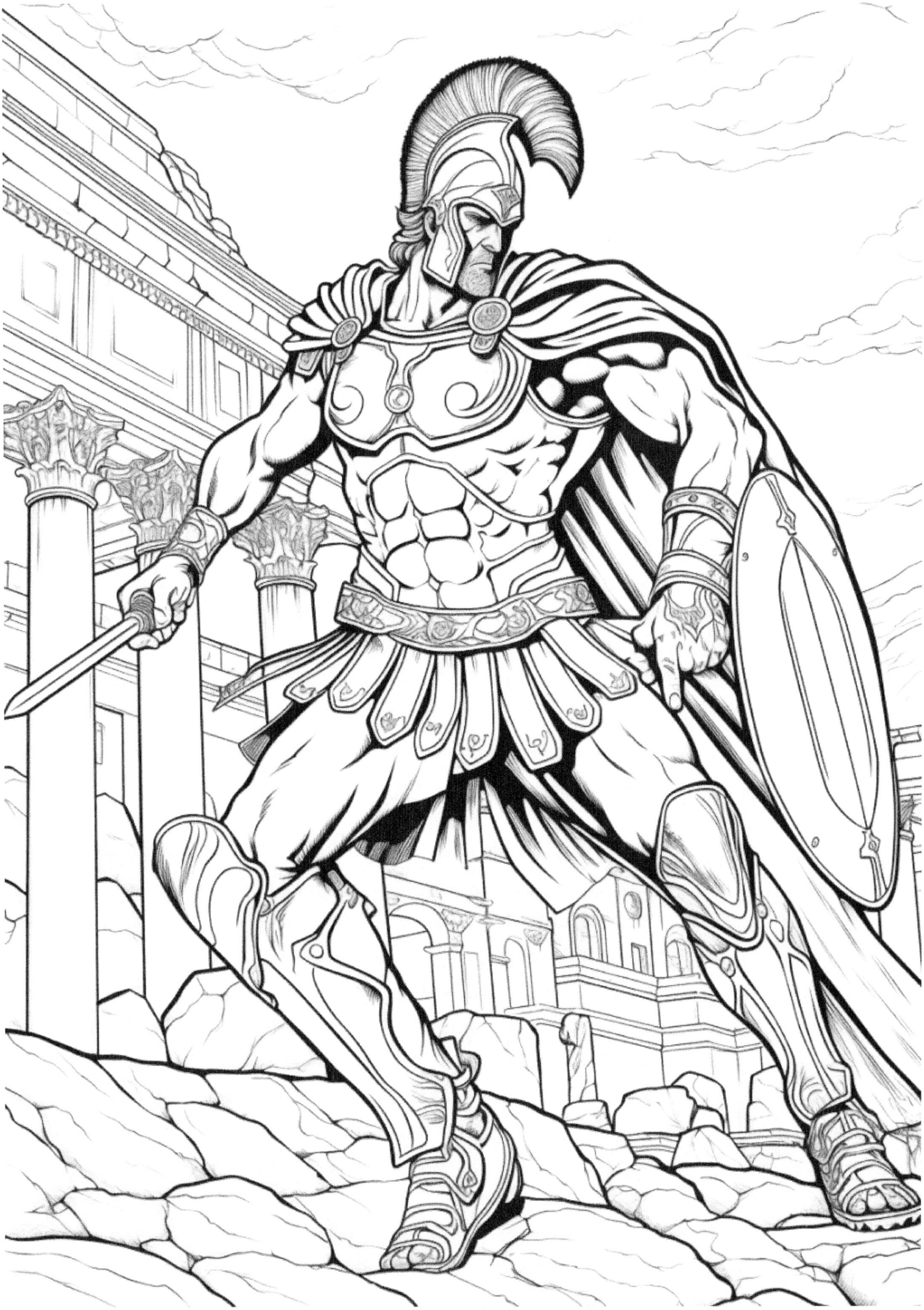

Apollo
God Of Music, Poetry, & Prophecy
Apollo and Daphne

In Greek mythology, the story of Apollo and Daphne begins with Eros, the mischievous god of love. Eros decides to intervene in the life of Apollo, the god of music and prophecy, to teach him a lesson. Eros shoots two arrows—one tipped with gold to inspire love and the other with lead to incite aversion.

One day, Apollo sees the beautiful nymph Daphne and is struck by the golden arrow, filling him with intense desire and love for her. However, Daphne is struck by the lead arrow, which makes her feel a strong aversion to love and commitment. She longs for freedom and independence.

Apollo, consumed by his newfound love, begins to pursue Daphne through the woods. He declares his affections and pleads for her to reciprocate his feelings, but Daphne resists. Despite her pleas and rejections, Apollo continues his relentless pursuit.

As Apollo draws closer, Daphne calls out to her father, the river god Peneus, for help. In response to her plea, Peneus transforms Daphne into a laurel tree to protect her from Apollo's grasp.

Apollo, devastated by the transformation of his beloved Daphne, embraces the laurel tree and declares it as a symbol of eternal devotion. He proclaims that the laurel tree will forever be associated with him and becomes a sacred symbol. Apollo adorns his head and lyre with laurel leaves, and laurel wreaths become a symbol of victory, honor, and the pursuit of beauty.

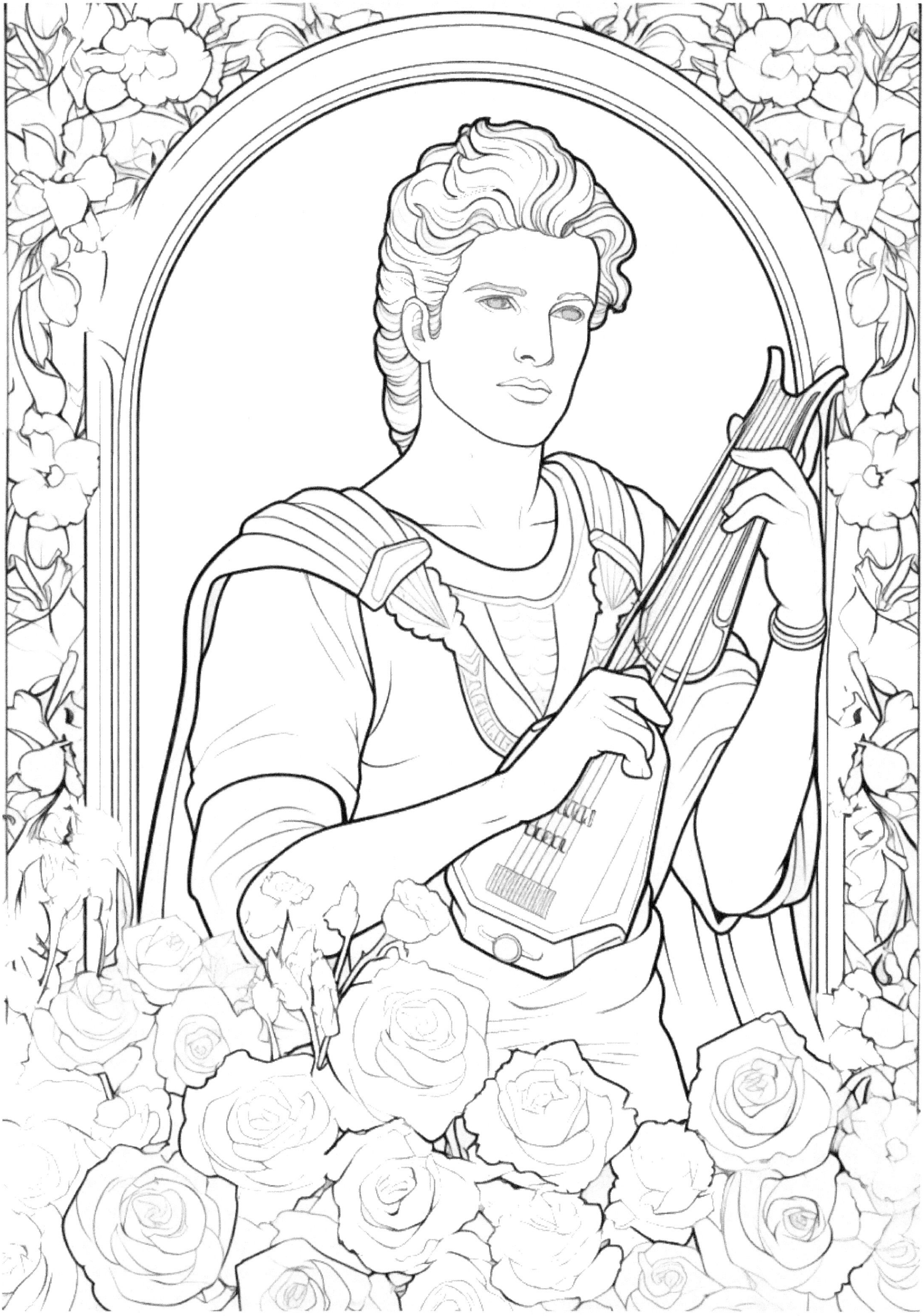

Ares
God Of War
Affair With Aphrodite

Ares, the Greek god of war, and Aphrodite, the goddess of love and beauty, found themselves irresistibly drawn to each other. Their passionate and tumultuous love affair became one of the most infamous in Greek mythology.

Aphrodite was married to Hephaestus, the god of blacksmiths, but her heart longed for the wild and fiery Ares. Ares, known for his fierce and impulsive nature, was equally enamoured by Aphrodite's allure and charm. They carried out their affair secretly, desperate to keep their forbidden love hidden from the eyes of the other gods.

However, their affair did not go unnoticed. Helios, the sun god, witnessed their secret meetings and informed Hephaestus of his wife's infidelity. Consumed by rage and hurt, Hephaestus devised a plan to expose the adulterous lovers.

Hephaestus skillfully crafted an invisible, fine-meshed net, known as the "unbreakable snare." He laid the trap around his marital bed, ensuring that Ares and Aphrodite would be ensnared in their passionate embrace. With the trap set, Hephaestus pretended to leave for an extended journey.

Ares, driven by desire, could not resist the opportunity to be with Aphrodite. They met in secret and became entwined in a passionate embrace on Hephaestus' bed. Little did they know that they were falling into Hephaestus' trap.

As the lovers lay together, the invisible net sprang to life, entangling them and rendering them helpless. The other gods were summoned, and a crowd gathered to witness the humiliation of Ares and Aphrodite. Laughter and mockery filled the room as the gods taunted the disgraced pair.

Aphrodite, ashamed and humiliated, pleaded for her release, but Hephaestus refused. It was only at the intervention of the god Hermes, who persuaded Hephaestus to release the lovers, that they were set free.

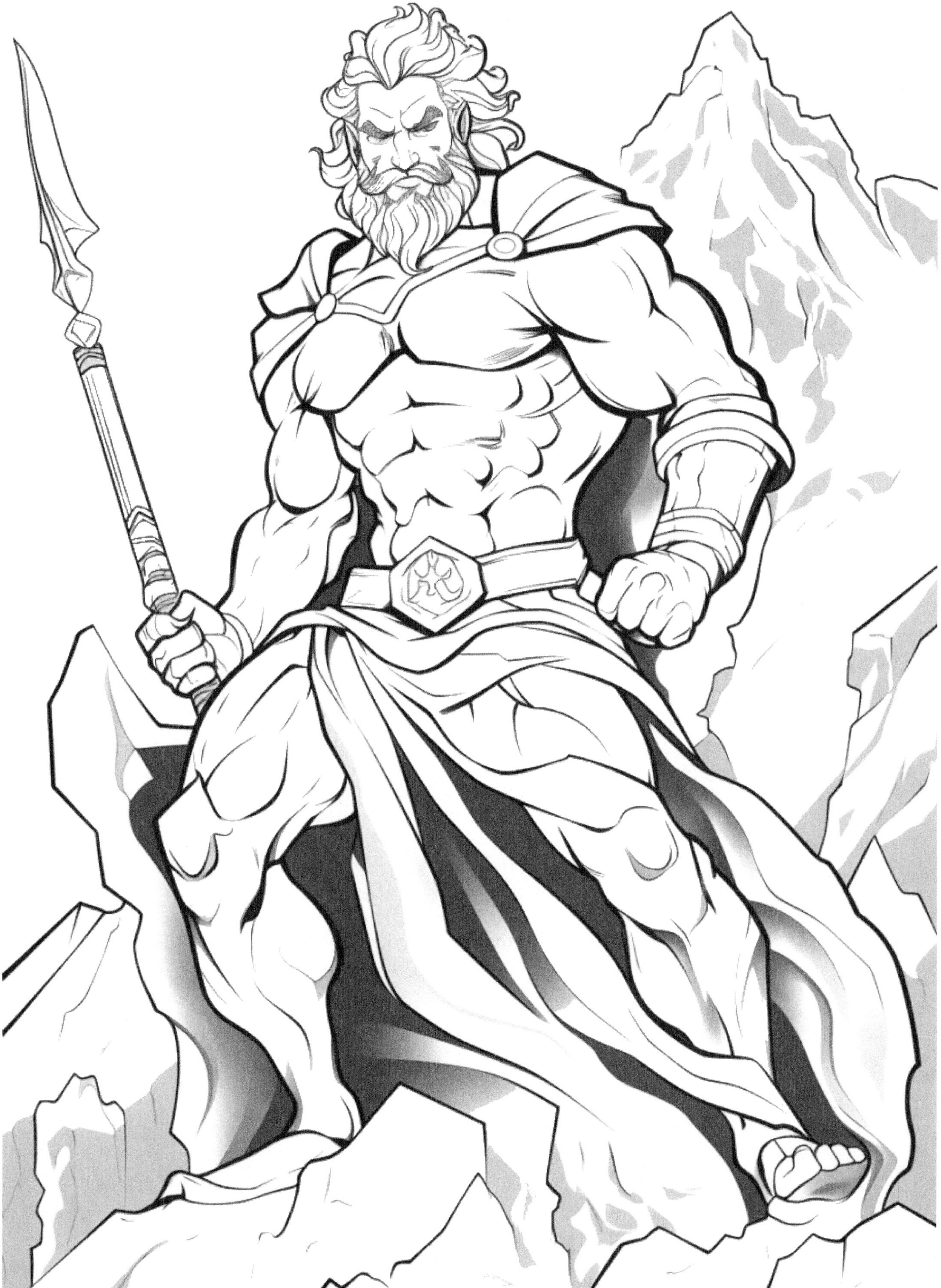

Diomedes
Hero Of The Trojan War
Diomedes & The Palladium

During the Trojan War, Diomedes, a courageous Greek hero, sought to weaken the defences of Troy. He learned of a sacred statue called the Palladium, believed to safeguard the city from destruction. Diomedes, accompanied by Odysseus, devised a plan to infiltrate Troy and steal the Palladium, hoping that its removal would bring an end to the Trojans' protection.

Disguised as Trojan soldiers, Diomedes and Odysseus sneaked into the heart of Troy under the cover of darkness. Guided by Athena, the goddess of wisdom and warfare, they navigated the city's streets undetected. Finally, they reached the temple where the Palladium was kept.

As Diomedes approached the statue, a supernatural aura surrounded it. According to the legend, the Palladium was an ancient wooden statue depicting the goddess Athena herself, said to have fallen from the heavens. Its presence was believed to ensure the security and prosperity of Troy.

Undeterred, Diomedes seized the statue, severing its divine protection from the Trojans. The theft went unnoticed until the next morning when the Trojans discovered the empty temple. Panic spread throughout the city as the realisation of the Palladium's disappearance sank in.

The stolen Palladium proved to be a significant turning point in the Trojan War. It weakened the Trojans' defences and bolstered the Greeks' confidence. With the Palladium in their possession, the Greeks were closer to achieving their ultimate goal—laying siege to Troy and bringing an end to the war

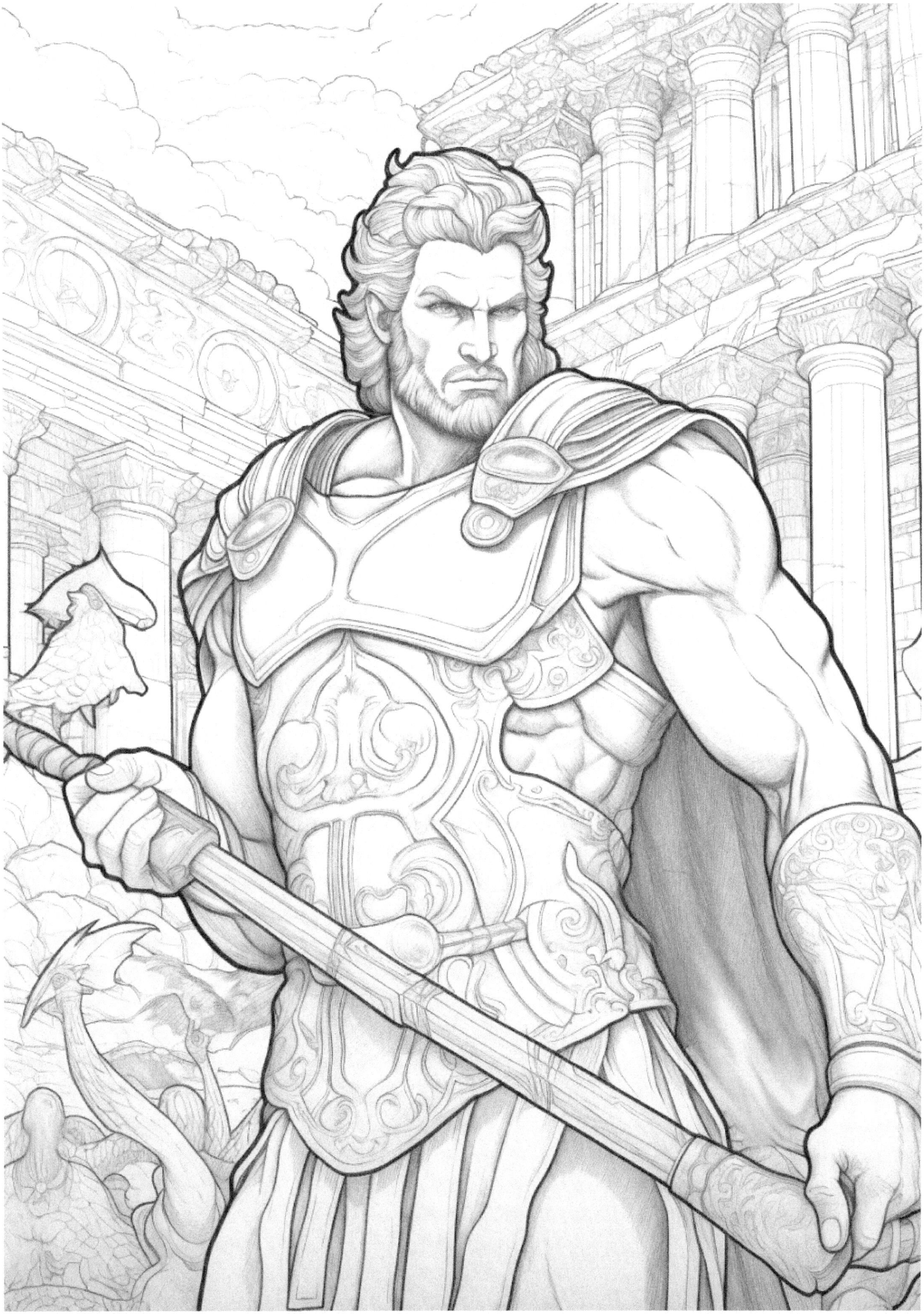

Medea
Sorceress & Enchantress
Medea's Revenge

After the quest for the Golden Fleece, Medea, the enchantress and wife of Jason, finds herself abandoned by her husband in Corinth. Jason plans to marry a Corinthian princess to solidify his political position, casting Medea aside. Consumed by anger, heartbreak, and a thirst for revenge, Medea sets in motion a series of events that will bring devastation.

Medea devises a cunning plan to exact her revenge on Jason. She presents a seemingly innocent gift to the Corinthian princess: a poisoned robe and a golden crown. The unsuspecting bride gratefully accepts the gifts and adorns herself with them. As soon as the garments touch her skin, an excruciating pain courses through her body. The poison spreads rapidly, causing her to writhe in agony. Her screams echo through the palace as she meets a gruesome fate.

But Medea's revenge does not stop there. Consumed by fury and wanting to ensure that Jason suffers as she has, she turns her attention to her own children. In a chilling act of desperation, Medea decides to kill her own sons. She justifies this monstrous act by claiming that it is an act of mercy, sparing them a life of pain and abandonment without their father's love.

With her children's blood on her hands, Medea escapes in a chariot drawn by fierce dragons, leaving behind a devastated Jason, who is left to grapple with the consequences of his actions.

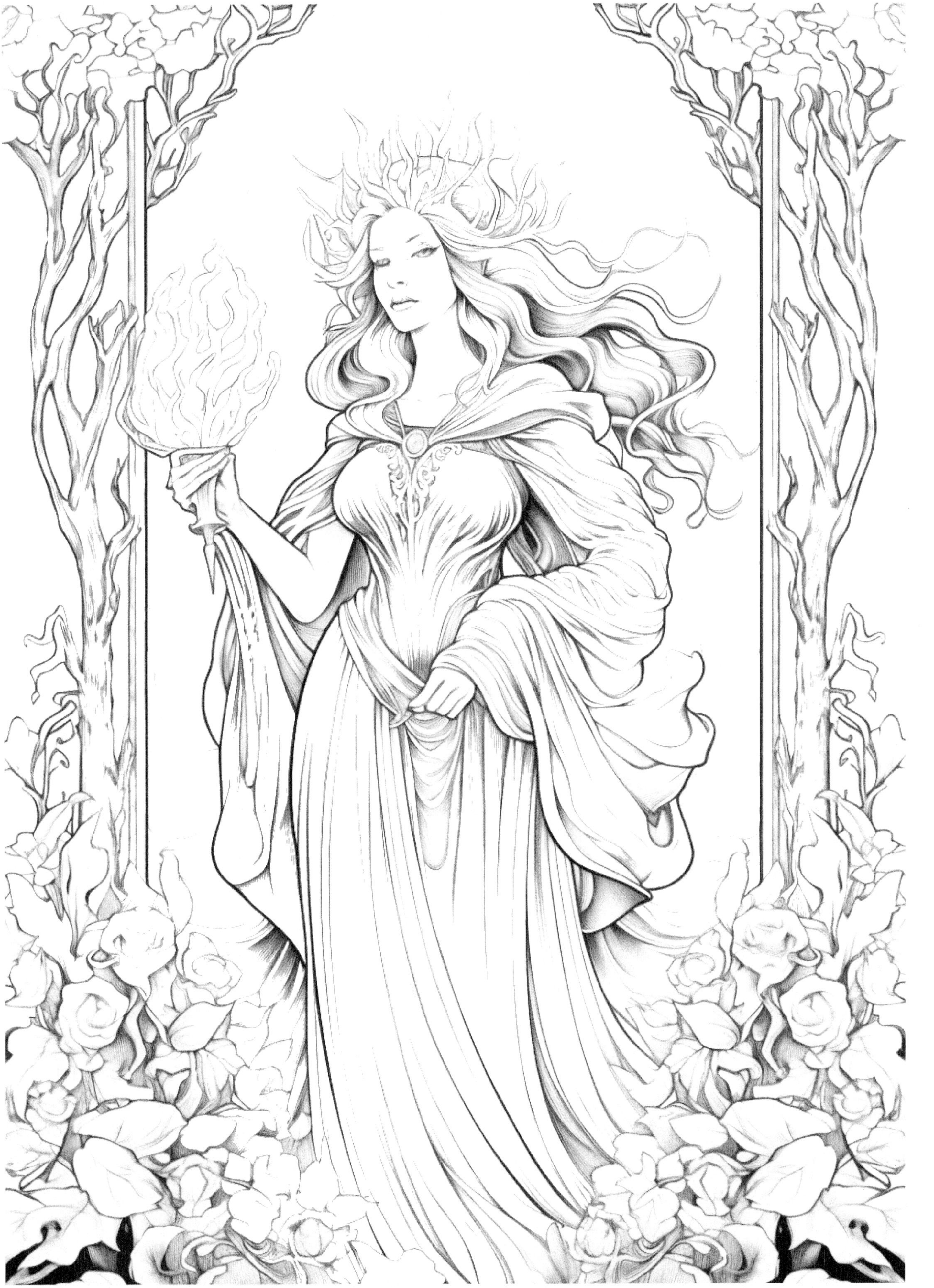

The Gorgon Medusa
Head Of Snakes & Petrifying Gaze
Perseus and the Gorgon Medusa

Perseus, the son of Zeus and Danae, was ordered by King Polydectes to bring him the head of Medusa, the most terrifying of the Gorgons. Medusa had snakes for hair and a gaze that could turn any mortal to stone.

With the help of the gods Hermes and Athena, Perseus set off on his quest. He received several gifts to aid him: a polished shield that acted as a mirror, a pair of winged sandals for swift flight, a helmet of invisibility, and a sickle-like sword from Zeus.

Guided by Athena, Perseus found the Gorgons' lair in a dark and distant cave. Using the reflective shield, he managed to avoid Medusa's gaze and cut off her head in a swift strike. As her blood spilled onto the ground, two creatures were born: the winged horse Pegasus and the giant Chrysaor.

With Medusa's head in his possession, Perseus used it as a powerful weapon. The mere sight of it turned enemies to stone. On his journey home, he encountered Andromeda, a princess chained to a rock as an offering to a sea monster. Perseus saved her by turning the monster to stone with Medusa's head.

Returning to Seriphos, Perseus revealed Medusa's head to King Polydectes during a banquet. The sight of the Gorgon turned the king and his guests to stone, punishing them for their ill intentions towards Perseus' mother.

Perseus then gifted Medusa's head to Athena, who placed it on her shield, the Aegis, as a symbol of her power.

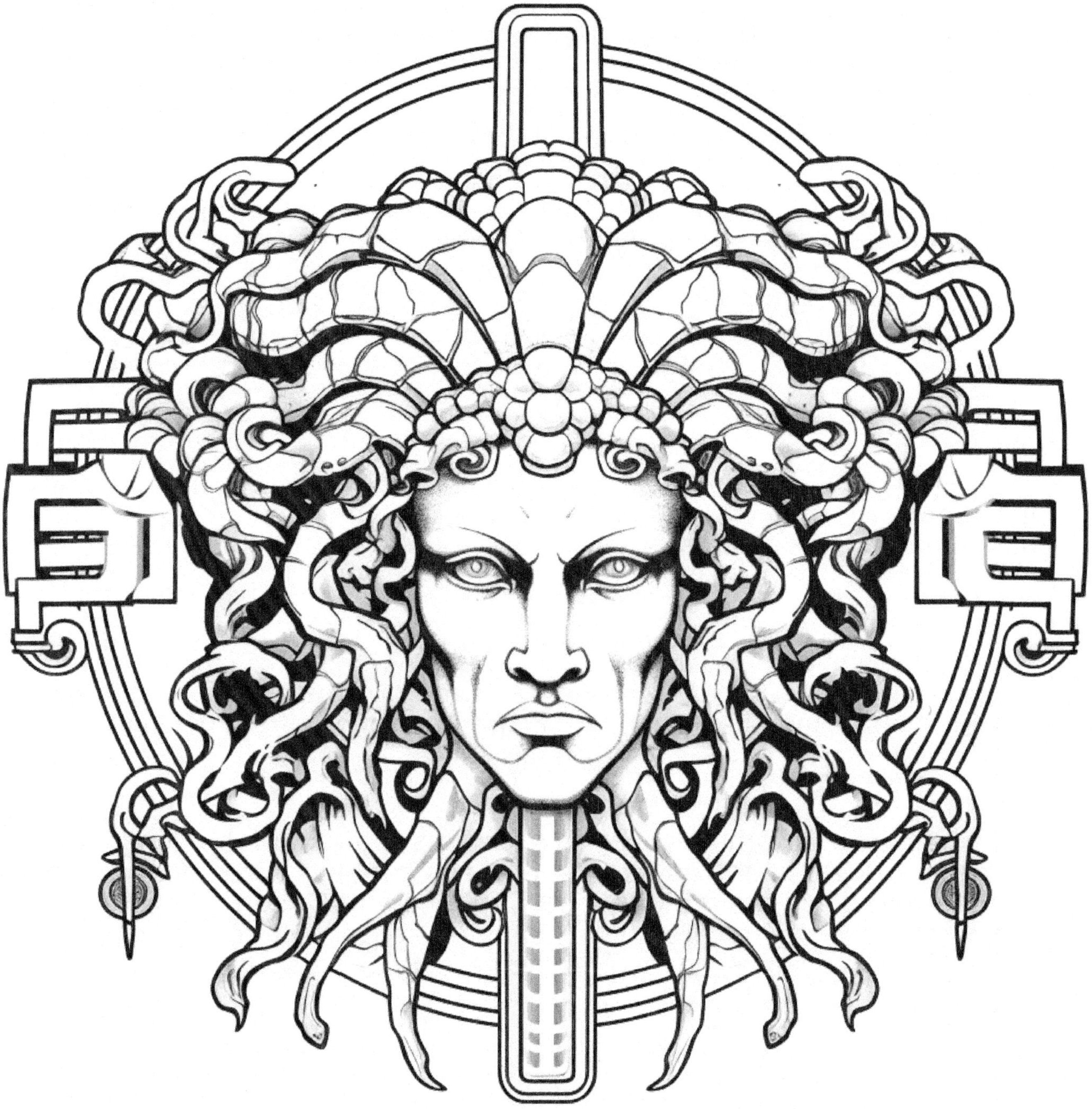

Perseus
Mythical Hero
The Andromeda Rescue

After slaying the Gorgon Medusa, Perseus embarked on further heroic adventures. During his journey, he came across the kingdom of Aethiopia, ruled by King Cepheus and Queen Cassiopeia. The kingdom was facing a terrible calamity as the sea monster, sent by the vengeful god Poseidon, was ravaging the coastal lands.

Queen Cassiopeia, in her vanity, had boasted that her daughter Andromeda was more beautiful than the Nereids, the sea nymphs. This angered Poseidon, who punished the kingdom by unleashing the fearsome sea monster upon its shores. In desperation, King Cepheus and Queen Cassiopeia consulted an oracle, which revealed that the only way to save their kingdom was to sacrifice Andromeda to the sea monster.

When Perseus heard of this unjust fate, he was determined to rescue Andromeda. He found her chained to a rock by the seashore, waiting to be devoured by the monster. Struck by her beauty and plight, Perseus vowed to save her.

Using his winged sandals to fly above the monster's reach, Perseus brandished the head of Medusa. The sight of Medusa's severed head turned the sea monster to stone, saving Andromeda from her perilous fate.

Perseus, now accompanied by Andromeda, returned to her kingdom where they were hailed as heroes. Perseus sought Andromeda's hand in marriage, and the grateful King Cepheus and Queen Cassiopeia agreed. The wedding ceremony was held in grandeur, celebrating the newfound peace and the heroics of Perseus.

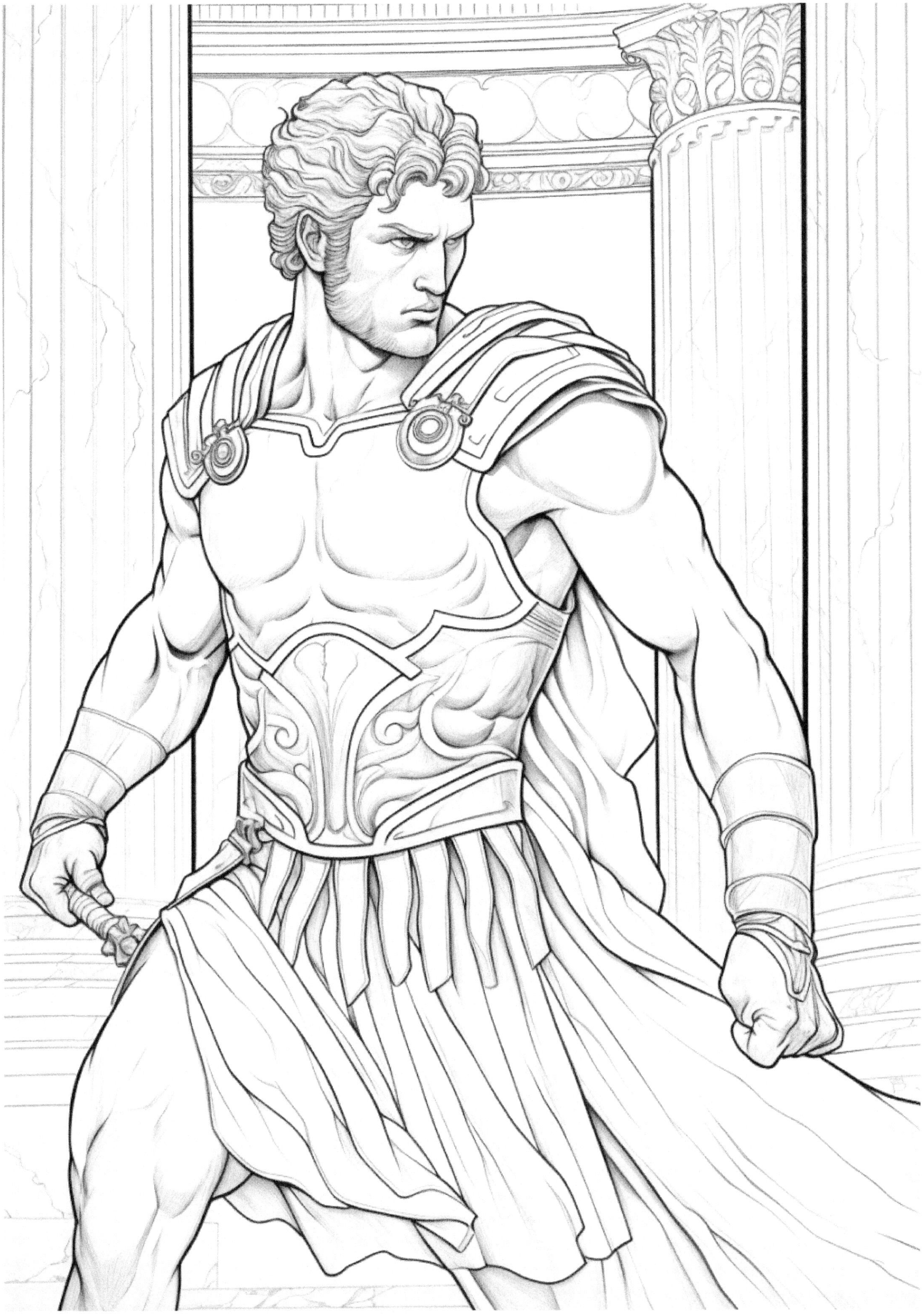

Poseidon
God Of The Sea & Earthquakes
The Creation Of The Horse

In Greek mythology, the creation of the horse is attributed to Poseidon, the god of the sea and earthquakes. The story begins with the grief-stricken goddess Demeter, who was mourning the abduction of her daughter Persephone by Hades, the god of the underworld.

To console Demeter, Poseidon decided to create a magnificent creature that would bring joy and wonder to both gods and mortals. He struck the earth with his mighty trident, causing the ground to split open and reveal a creature of unparalleled beauty and strength—the horse.

From the fissure emerged a majestic animal with a flowing mane, powerful hooves, and a sleek body. Its grace and speed captivated everyone who laid eyes upon it. The horse quickly became a symbol of power, freedom, and untamed beauty.

Poseidon bestowed upon the horse a spirit that matched its physical magnificence. He gifted it with swiftness, endurance, and an indomitable spirit, making it an ideal companion for mortals. The horse became a loyal and invaluable partner to humans, aiding them in transportation, agriculture, and warfare.

The creation of the horse had a significant impact on Greek culture. Horses played a crucial role in Greek mythology and history, particularly in the context of the Trojan War. The Greek warriors, known as the Achaeans, utilised their mastery of horsemanship to their advantage, employing horses as a strategic asset in battle.

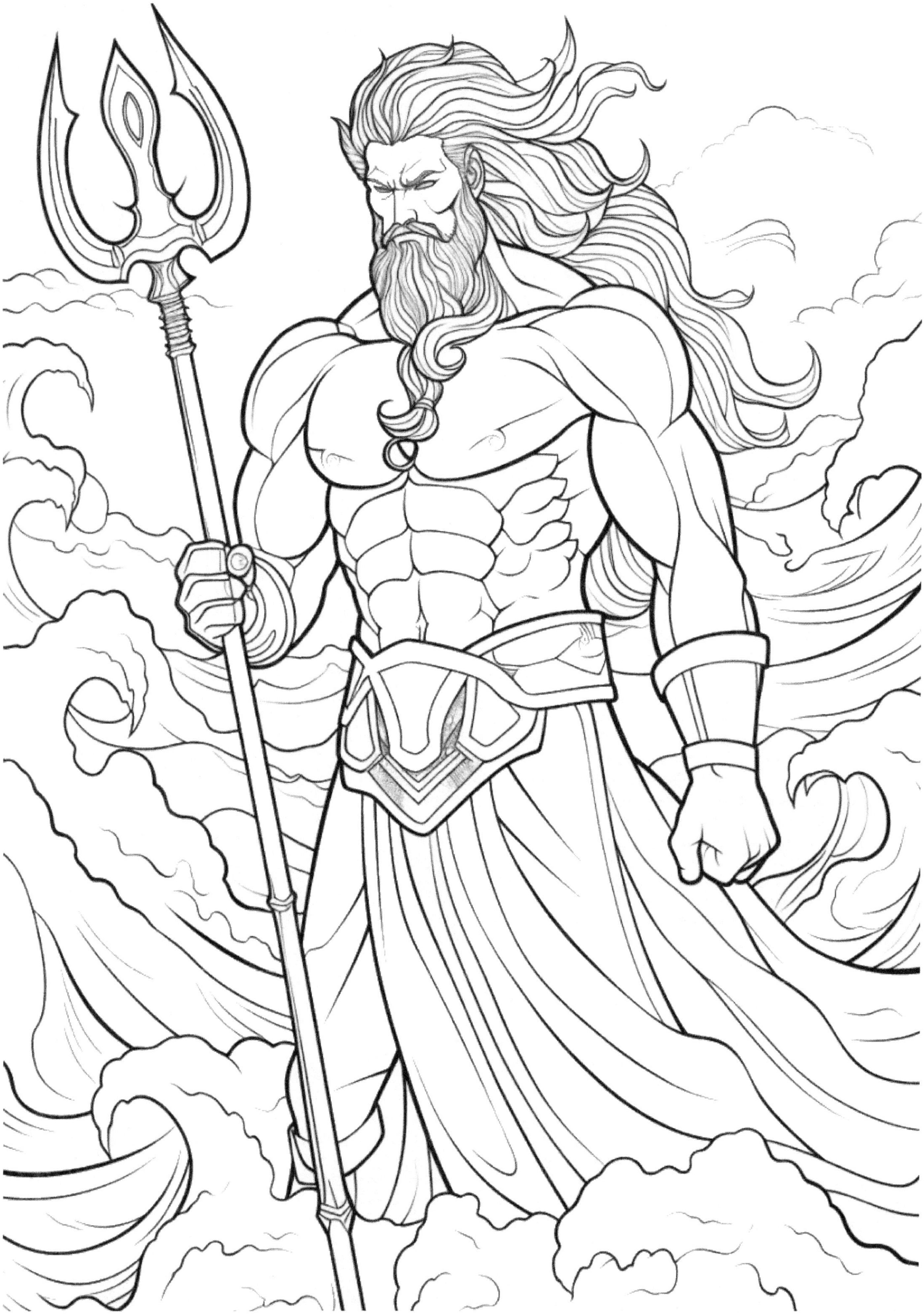

Jason
Legendary Greek Hero
Jason & The Argonaugts

Jason, in the myth of Jason and the Argonauts, was a hero and the leader of the Argonauts—a band of legendary Greek heroes who embarked on a perilous journey aboard the ship Argo in search of the Golden Fleece. Jason was the son of Aeson, the rightful king of Iolcus, but his throne was usurped by his wicked uncle, Pelias.

To reclaim his rightful place, Jason set out on a quest to retrieve the Golden Fleece, a symbol of kingship and prosperity. He assembled a crew of heroes, including Hercules, Theseus, and Orpheus, and sailed on the ship Argo, hence earning the name "Argonauts."

Their journey was fraught with challenges and dangers, including encounters with mythical creatures, treacherous seas, and cunning sorceresses. Jason displayed leadership, bravery, and intelligence as he navigated these obstacles, relying on the help of his companions and the favour of the gods.

Upon reaching Colchis, the land where the Golden Fleece was kept, Jason faced another daunting task. The fleece was guarded by a dragon that never slept. With the aid of Medea, a sorceress and princess of Colchis who fell in love with Jason, he devised a plan to defeat the dragon and claim the Golden Fleece.

With the Golden Fleece in their possession, Jason and the Argonauts sailed back to Iolcus. Their return was accompanied by further trials, including the curse of Medea's vengeance against Pelias, which led to the downfall of Pelias and the restoration of Jason's father as the rightful king.

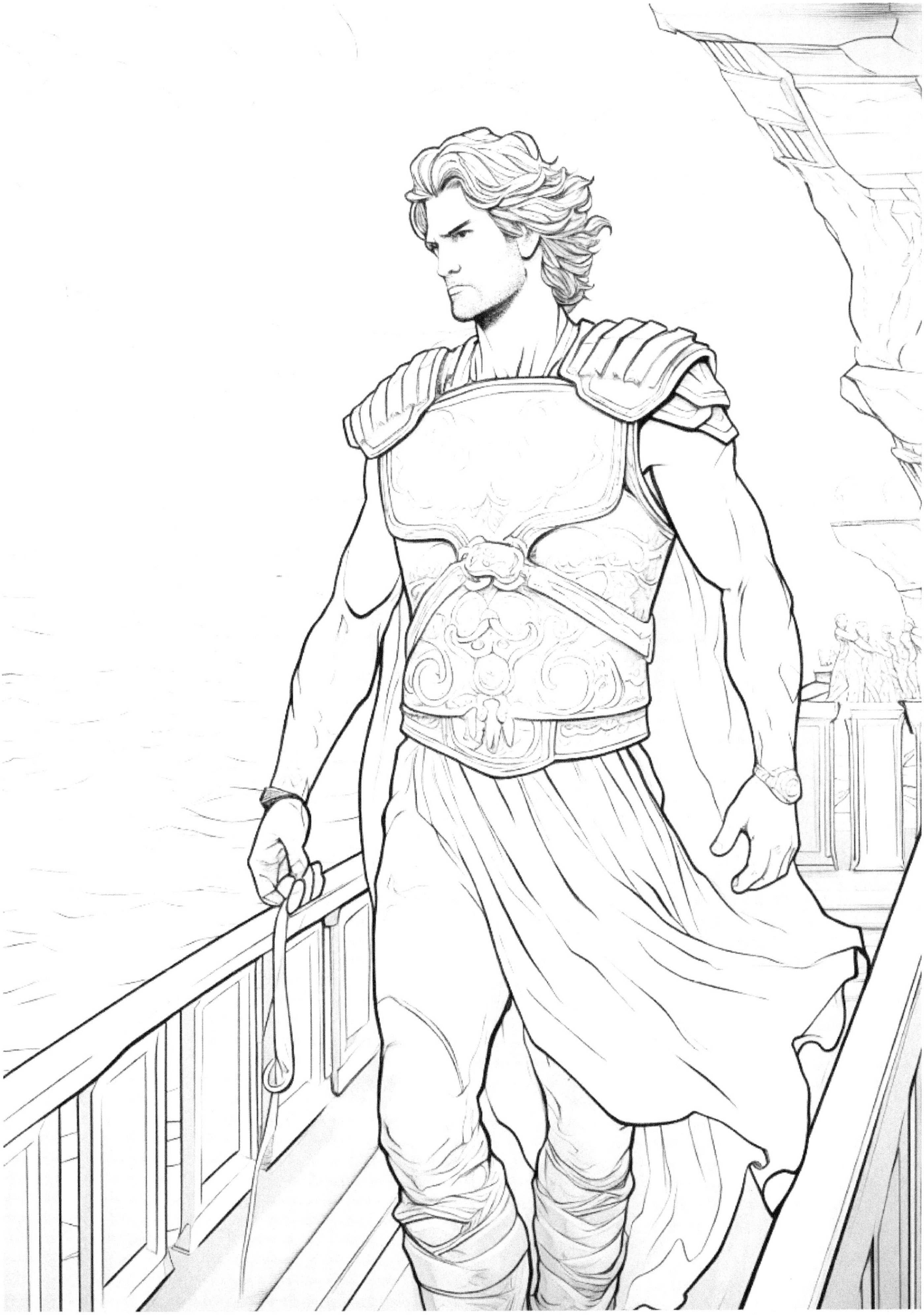

Hydra
Regenerating Mythical Monster
Jason & The Hydra's Teeth

During Jason's quest for the Golden Fleece, one of the challenges he encountered was the task of obtaining the golden fleece from the kingdom of Colchis. To aid him in this task, he sought the guidance of King Aeetes, who set him on a seemingly impossible mission: to sow the teeth of a dragon, known as the Hydra, and defeat the warriors that sprouted from the ground.

Undeterred by the daunting task, Jason ventured into the field and followed King Aeetes' instructions. He carefully sowed the dragon's teeth into the soil and watched in awe as armed men sprang forth from the earth. These warriors, known as the Spartoi, were fearsome and ready for battle.

Recognising the danger, Jason quickly devised a clever plan. Instead of engaging the Spartoi in direct combat, he remembered the advice of the sorceress Medea, who had fallen in love with him. Medea had provided him with a magical ointment that granted him temporary invulnerability.

Jason applied the ointment to his body, rendering him impervious to harm. As the Spartoi attacked, their weapons proved futile against him. Confusion and discord spread among the warriors as they turned on each other, unable to harm Jason.

Taking advantage of the chaos, Jason swiftly defeated the remaining Spartoi, their numbers dwindling with each passing moment. His quick thinking and the aid of Medea's magic allowed him to emerge victorious from the deadly encounter.

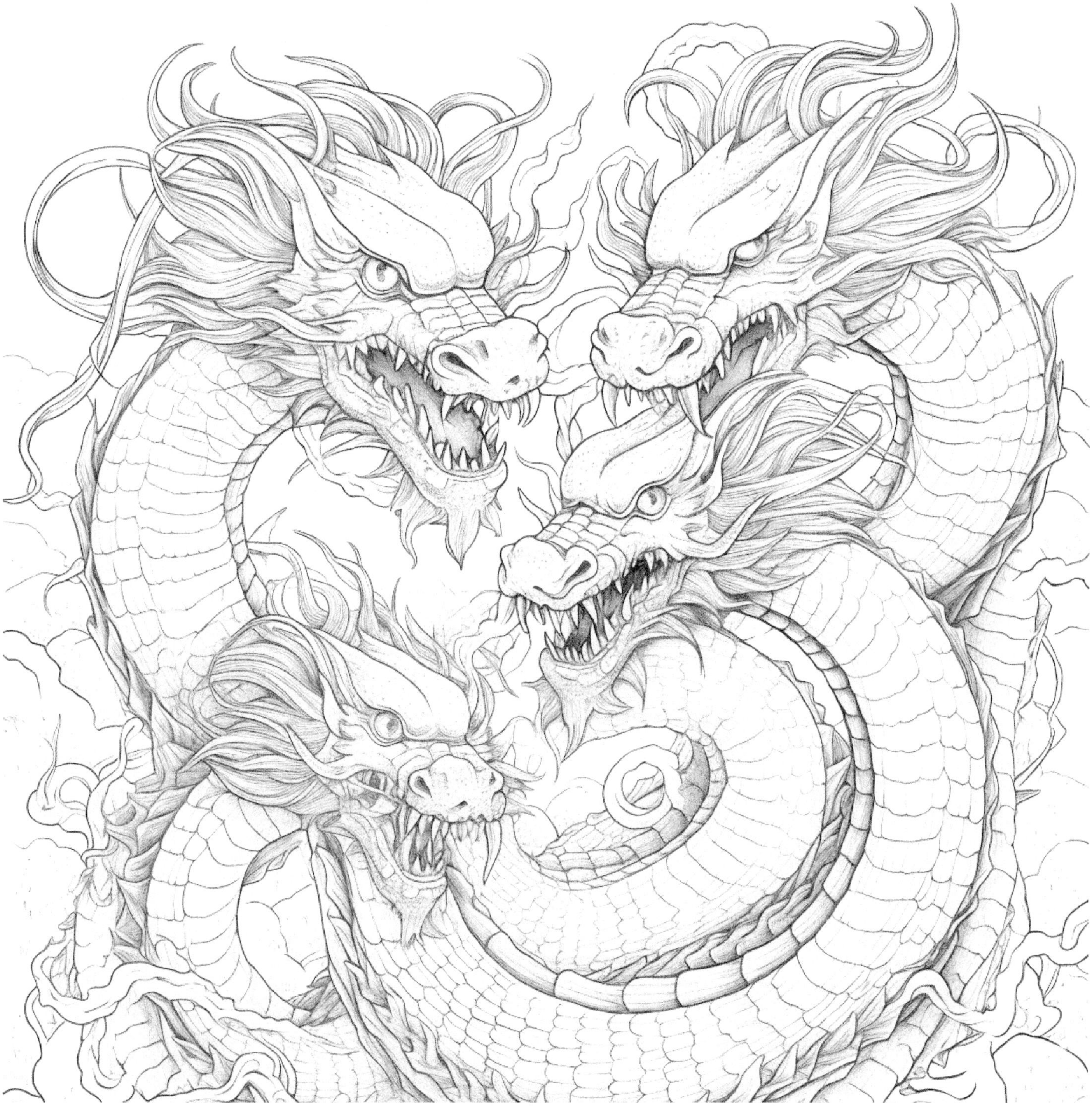

Jason
Legendary Greek Hero
Crossing the Clashing Rocks

As Jason and his crew sailed on the Argo in their quest for the Golden Fleece, they encountered a treacherous obstacle known as the Clashing Rocks. These enormous cliffs were said to be alive, relentlessly smashing together and crushing any ship that dared to pass through.

Desperate to continue their journey, Jason sought the guidance of Phineus, a blind prophet who possessed knowledge of the Clashing Rocks. Phineus advised Jason on the precise timing required to navigate through the perilous passage. He warned that only a truly skilled helmsman could guide the ship safely through the narrow gap between the rocks.

Armed with this invaluable knowledge, Jason prepared his crew for the dangerous task ahead. As the Argo approached the Clashing Rocks, tension filled the air. Every heartbeat seemed to amplify the crew's anxiety.

With unwavering determination, Jason took the helm and steered the ship through the treacherous passage. The crew, on high alert, watched in awe as the massive cliffs started to close in. Just as it seemed impossible to escape the impending doom, Jason skillfully manoeuvred the Argo with precise timing.

At the last moment, when it appeared that all was lost, the Clashing Rocks suddenly halted, freezing in place. The Argo sailed through the narrow gap unscathed, leaving the rocks behind.

The crew let out a collective sigh of relief and cheered their victory. They had successfully overcome one of the most perilous challenges of their journey, thanks to Jason's skill and the guidance of Phineus.

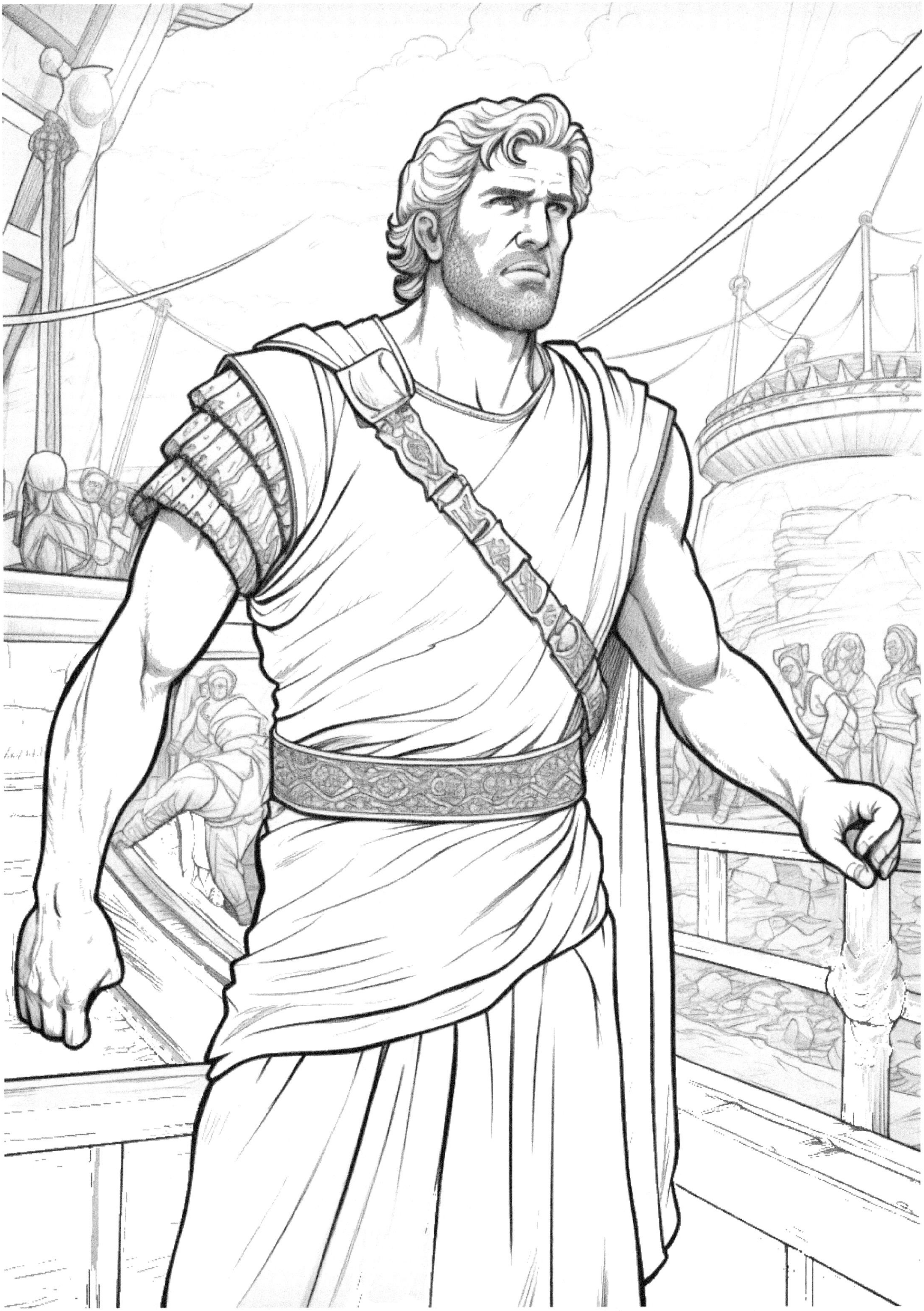

Theseus
Legendary Greek Hero
Theseus and the Minotaur

In ancient Greek mythology, King Minos of Crete demanded a tribute of seven Athenian youths and seven maidens every nine years to be sacrificed to the Minotaur, a monstrous creature with the body of a man and the head of a bull. Theseus, the brave son of King Aegeus of Athens, volunteered to be one of the young Athenians and vowed to put an end to the terror of the Minotaur.

Upon arriving in Crete, Theseus caught the attention of Princess Ariadne, King Minos' daughter. Ariadne fell in love with Theseus and decided to help him in his quest. She provided him with a ball of thread and instructed him to unravel it as he ventured into the labyrinth, allowing him to find his way back.

Entering the dark and winding labyrinth, Theseus followed the thread's path until he reached the heart of the maze where the Minotaur lurked. With courage and determination, Theseus confronted the fearsome creature. Armed with a sword, he fought valiantly and managed to slay the Minotaur, ending its reign of terror.

Following his victory, Theseus retraced his steps with the aid of the thread, leading him back to the entrance of the labyrinth. He escaped Crete, taking Princess Ariadne with him as his companion and love.

However, tragedy struck as Theseus forgot to hoist the white sail on his return voyage, a prearranged signal for his successful mission. Seeing the black sail, King Aegeus, in despair, believed his son to be dead and threw himself into the sea, which came to be known as the Aegean Sea.

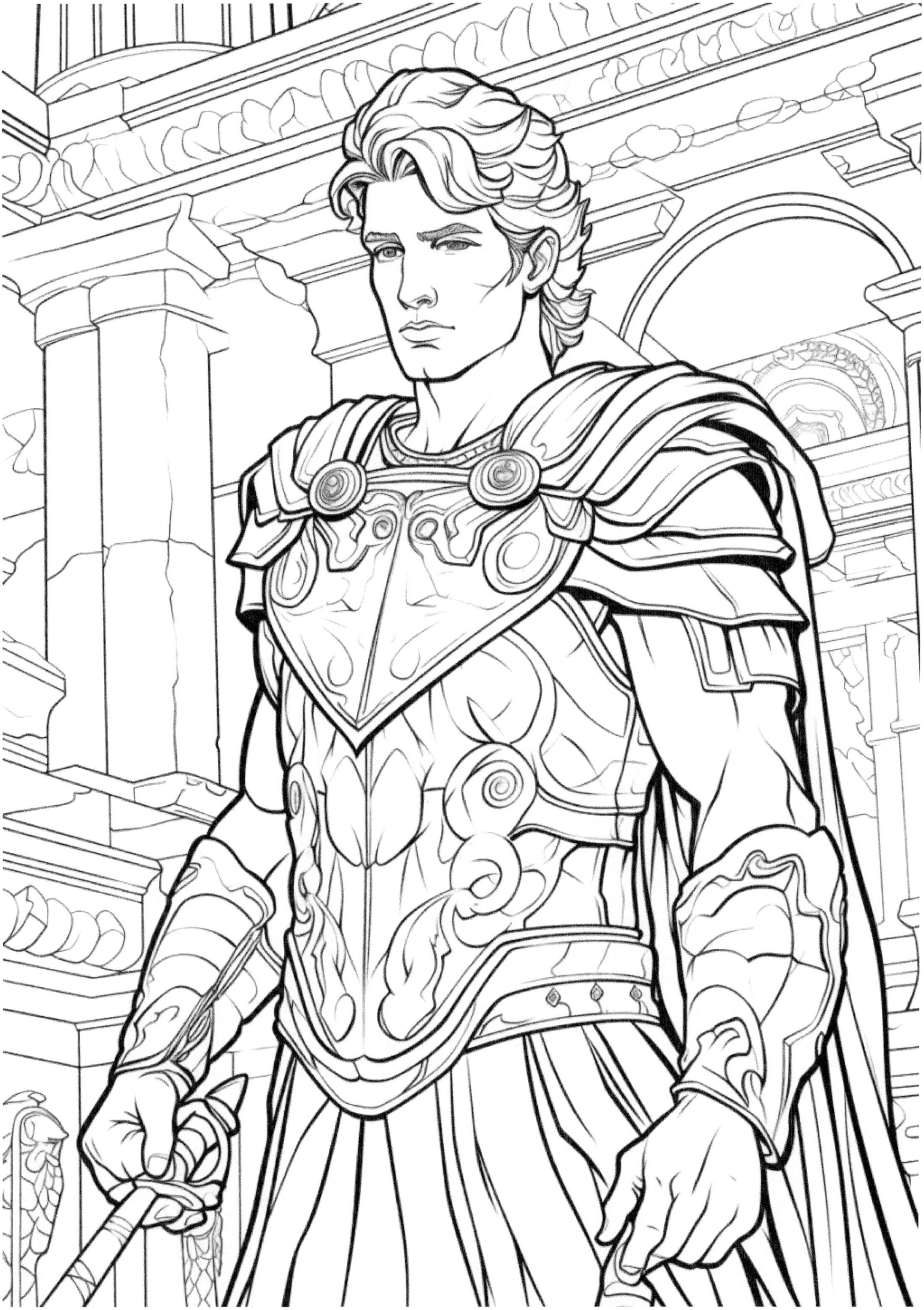

Charybdis & Scylla
Monsters Of The Deep
The Odyssey

In Homer's epic poem "The Odyssey," the hero Odysseus and his crew encountered the treacherous waters inhabited by both Charybdis and Scylla. As they sailed through the narrow strait between them, Odysseus faced a difficult choice. Charybdis, a massive whirlpool, threatened to swallow their entire ship, while Scylla, a fearsome six-headed monster, lurked on a nearby rock. Aware of the dangers, Odysseus decided to navigate closer to Scylla's side, sacrificing a few men to her monstrous appetite rather than risking the entire crew to the swirling depths of Charybdis.

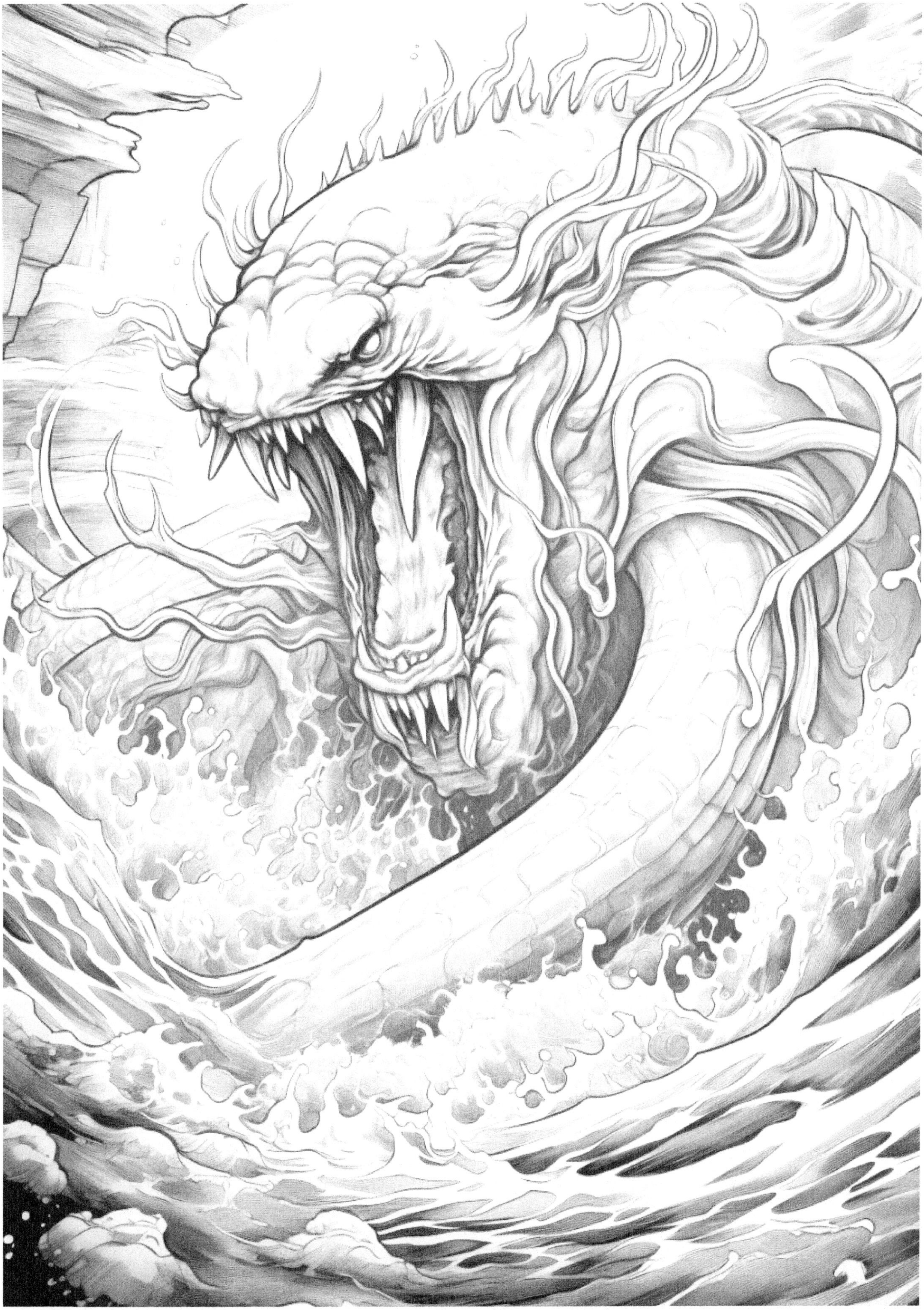

Printed in Great Britain
by Amazon